Cropley, A.J.

More Ways Than One: Fostering
Creativity in the Classroom

Creativity Research

Mark A. Runco, Series Editor

Achieving Extraordinary Ends: An Essay on Creativity, by Sharon Bailin
Counseling Gifted and Talented Children, edited by Roberta M. Milgram
Creative Thinking: Problem-Solving Orientation and the Arts Orientation, by John F. Wakefield
Divergent Thinking, by Mark A. Runco
More Ways Than One: Fostering Creativity, by Arthur J. Cropley
Perspectives on Creativity: The Biographical Method, by John E. Gedo and Mary M. Gedo

In Preparation:

Beyond Terman: Longitudinal Studies in Contemporary Gifted Education, edited by Karen Arnold and Rena Subotnick
Contexts of Creativity, by Leonora Cohen, Amit Goswami, Shawn Boles, and Richard Chaney
Creativity: Theories, Themes and Issues, by Mark A. Runco
Creativity and Affect, edited by Melvin Shaw and Klaus Hoppe
Creativity in Government, by Thomas Heinzen
Genius Revisited: High IQ Children Grown Up, by Rena Subotnik, Lee Kassan, Ellen Summers, and Alan Wasser
Nuturing and Developing Creativity: Emergence of a Discipline, Volume 2, edited by Scot G. Isaksen, Mary C. Murdock, Roger L. Firestien, and Donald J. Treffinger
Problem Finding, Problem Solving, and Creativity, edited by Mark A Runco
Understanding and Recognizing Creativity: Emergence of a Discipline, Volume 1, edited by Scott G. Isaksen, Mary C. Murdock, Roger L. Firestien, and Donald J. Treffinger

MORE WAYS THAN ONE: FOSTERING CREATIVITY

Arthur J. Cropley

University of Hamburg

ABLEX PUBLISHING CORPORATION
NORWOOD, NEW JERSEY

Printed in the United States of America

Ablex Publishing Corporation
P.O. Box 5297
Greenwich, Connecticut 06830

Contents

Foreword

In *More Ways than One*, Professor Cropley offers a scholarly—but highly prgamatic—view of creativity and its cultivation. Cropley reviews and evaluates a great deal of research, and carefully explores the numerous practical implications of that work. The research spans 50 years, and includes Cropley's own work—and he has been producing sound contributions on this topic since the 1960s. The topics in *More Ways than One* are all relevant to education, but not limited to conventional academic concerns. Cropley covers giftedness, educational equality, and play, for example, but also offers discussions of creativity and health, "blocks within society," and the value of creativity for society. The range of topics in *More Ways than One* is impressive, as is the balance of basic and applied thought.

This monograph is also good reading in that Cropley presents the research and his views in a variety of ways: He reviews and evaluates research; he shares personal experiences and anecdotes; he presents case studies; and here and there he offers concepts which are quite provocative as well as useful. The concept of *creative style* is, for instance, a very important one, for it suggests that there are particular processes and behaviors which can—but do not necessarily—lead to a truly creative product. This can be taken as a reminder that the means are more important than the ends, and that the process is more important than the end product. Educators will appreciate this for it suggests that we can encourage the creative thinking and behavior patterns of *every* child. To bring this point home, Cropley offers a convincing argument about *the learning advantage of creativity*. This advantage can be given to every child. This is especially the case because, as Cropley notes early in the monograph, creativity is not a purely cognitive phenomenon. Rather, it has cognitive, motivational, and emotional bases. Creativity is not something only the brightest can do or have.

Although this monograph was prepared especially for Ablex's *Creativity Research Monograph Series*, portions of it are based on material which was originally published in German. This is relevant for two reasons. First, Ehrenwirth Verlag is to be thanked for granting permission to use this material. Second, this helps to explain why the monograph contains such a sound foundation of background research—research which is international, and which has evolved over a 50-year period.

As I see it, *More Ways than One* validates much of the research on creativity. Granted, validation typically comes through carefully conducted correlational research. But in this book, Cropley demonstrates how research can be applied. I believe that if research findings have clear applicability, they have value. Isn't value one indicator of validity? It is a validation through application. *More Ways than One* is an excellent addition to the *Creativity Research Monograph Series*.

Mark A. Runco

1

Purposes, Method, and Orientation

GOALS OF THE BOOK

Educational Philosophy and Aim

In the past, both society and teachers have had an unnecessarily narrow view of children's thinking processes in general, and of giftedness in particular. Recent studies confirming this in international settings are reported by Howieson (1984) and Obuche (1986). As a result of the narrow view, inventive and innovative capacities have been undervalued in favor of recognition, recall, and reapplication of existing knowledge. This book introduces a broader understanding of intellectual giftedness and encourages teachers to value a more varied set of skills, concentrating particularly on innovation, novelty, discovery, and the like. Techniques and approaches for fostering venturesome and inventive thinking in the classroom are suggested. This book does not, however, provide a set of readymade answers or a precise blueprint for teachers to follow but presents general guidelines that they may use in order to develop their own methods.

The Purpose of the Book

It is hoped that the book will encourage parents and educators to think more broadly about human intelligence and help them to achieve a highly practical understanding of its applications, particularly by extending it to encompass the nebulous concept of creativity. It is also important, and perhaps especially important for creativity, that teachers become explicitly aware of the emotional and motivational basis of learning and thinking so that they do not concentrate only on its cognitive aspects. Consequently, it is hoped that the book will encourage a fuller understanding of the broad range of classroom factors that affect both conventional and creative thinking. It is also hoped that teachers will expand their own innovative and creative capacities and use these to develop their own techniques and materials. Finally, it is hoped that they will ultimately encourage more flexible and inventive thinking on the part of their students.

Organization of the Material

The book contains three kinds of material. The first consists of conclusions and generalizations based on a body of empirical data from research studies in various countries. The second consists of opinions, advice, and suggestions deriving from the author's own knowledge and experience. The final kind involves anecdotes giving examples of what are regarded as good or bad classroom practice. Most of these "cautionary tales" are real-life stories from real people's school experiences, told to me by adults reminiscing about their teachers.

RESEARCH ON CREATIVITY

Research on creativity is by no means new. In his *Ion*, Plato concluded that it results from inspiration by the gods. Chinese researchers in about 100 BC conducted one of the first studies on the fostering of creative giftedness. In an experimental group-control group study they compared "special education" at the emperor's court with education at home. Over 2,000 years later, a second Chinese study (Zha, 1986) again emphasized the importance of the environment in promoting the development of gifted children. Classical case study investigations in the first half of the 20th century were presented by Freud (1910), Wallas (1926), and Hadamard (1945), and Lehman began his biographical research on scientific creativity and age about 60 years ago (e.g., Lehman & Witty, 1931). Research methods may be divided into three broad categories: biographical and autobiographical studies, investigations based on test scores (see discussions of "creativity" tests in a later section), and experimental studies. These three areas often overlap. Consider, for instance, the historical studies in which IQs of famous creators were estimated (Cox, 1926), or experimental investigations in which test scores constituted independent or dependent variables. Nonetheless, the division into categories is helpful.

The most frequent application of the biographical method has involved retrospective case studies of famous creative achievers in the arts and sciences (e.g., Cox, 1926; Hadamard, 1945; Lehman, 1953). More recently, unusually creative specialists in a number of areas—architecture, for instance—have been identified by asking colleagues or experts to nominate particularly creative members of their areas of specialization. Subsequently, the persons nominated have been studied, sometimes very intensively, usually by means of some combination of interviews, self-descriptions, tests, observation during the solving of problems, and analysis of published works or other achievements. "Classic" studies are those of Barron (1963) with air force officers, Roe (1952) with scientists and mathematicians, MacKinnon (1983) with architects, Helson (1983) with female mathematicians, and Drevdahl and Cattell (1958) with artists and writers. These studies all concentrated heavily on the role of personality in creativity. Gardner (1988) discussed the advantages of the case study method in identifying giftedness and called for "cognitive case studies." An example of what this might involve is to be found in Hendrickson's (1986) longitudinal case studies (although she did not confine herself to the cognitive area) of four gifted Australian violinists who were followed over a period of several years. The study began at about the time they began to take lessons and continued until they became accomplished or even world-famous players.

Also relatively common are self-report studies in which famous creators have described the way in which they thought their achievements had occurred (see Ghiselin, 1952, for a summary). Simonton (1988) pointed out that the investigators in such studies sometimes (in his opinion, frequently) twist the contents of self-reports to make them conform to preconceived models, rather than allowing the models to emerge from the materials. Weisberg (1986) raised further doubts about the value of self-reports by drawing attention to discrepancies between objective facts and the claims of some subjects. He concluded, for instance, that neither the stage of "incubation" described by Wallas (1926), nor the almost mystical "aha experience" described by many famous creative people, exists.

The simplest test-linked studies define *creativity* as a score on a test and then examine correlations with other scores (e.g., IQs, scores on personality tests, etc.) or with school grades, scores on rating scales, and the like. Studies of this kind predominate in education (see McLeod & Cropley, 1989, for examples). Less common are longitudinal studies, although several such investigations of creativity test scores and school achievement/out of school achievement exist (Cropley, 1972; Howieson, 1981; Torrance, 1980; Wallach & Wing, 1969). Among the approaches which have been applied in experimental studies are story telling (Hennessey & Amabile, 1988), construction of thinking aloud protocols (Clement, 1989), tachistoscopic exposure of stimulus objects (Smith & Carlsson, 1989), and manipulation of visual imagery (Rothenberg, 1988, 1990). In Rothenberg's research, subjects were asked to construct a new poetic metaphor under differing conditions: during exposure to slides depicting "poetic" themes either singly (simple stimulus), for example, or superimposed on each other (complex stimulus).

An outstanding example of research involving an eclectic approach is Rothenberg's (1983) study of what he called "janusian" thinking. His subjects were 12 Nobel-prize-winning scientists, 18 schizophrenic patients, and 113 college students, divided on the basis of test scores into high and low creative groups. Thinking style was measured by means of timed word association tests. He showed that the scientists and the highly creative students resembled each other cognitively but differed from the noncreatives. This was also true of the schizophrenics. However, the creative individuals did not show thinking processes similar to those of schizophrenics. As a result, it could be concluded that creativity is related to atypical ways of thinking, but these were not the same as the aberrational thinking of psychotics (see later discussions of creativity and mental illness).

PERSONAL THOUGHTS ON CLASSROOM CREATIVITY

A great deal of the content of this book involves summarizing and coordinating a body of empirical findings and opinions. The way in which this has been done necessarily reflects my personal views. However, these views are usually implicit rather than explicit. The following section states more directly a number of personal opinions about several key issues.

Confusion About What Creativity Is

Many parents and teachers have expressed concern, in recent years, not that there is inadequate emphasis on creative thinking in the classroom, but that there is too much! Proponents of creativity seem to have gone too far. Critics draw attention to teachers' tolerance of selfish, undisciplined, and careless or lazy behavior. Much of this tolerance or even active encouragement is justified by those who support it on the grounds that it fosters creativity, without any evidence that it really does. It may well be that many of the complaints of the critics are justified. Kneller (1965) discussed the problem of creativity becoming a catchall term, as did Nicholls (1972). Nonetheless, as Brown (1977) pointed out, many famous creative breakthroughs have had illogical aspects.

Unfortunately, some people recognized as being creative have encouraged a "do-as-you-like" school of thought by reporting that their creativity involved little or no real effort on their part. Indeed, in the early stages there was strong opposition to modern attempts to study creativity in a formal manner, on the grounds that it is essentially a spiritual phenomenon, and therefore above systematic analysis. Ghiselin (1952) gave many examples of famous creators—including Shelley, Blake, Henry James, Spencer, Nietzsche, and Gauss—who reported that their creativity came, as it were, "automatically." Poincaré reported that his creative mathematical breakthrough occurred to him more or less complete in a dream. However, examination of the work histories of acknowledged creative people, even those who reported that it all happened in a flash of inspiration, suggests that they have overlooked the hard work that went into their creativity, perhaps because it was more gratifying to see themselves as the earthly agents of cosmic forces than as hard workers. As a result, creativity seems frequently to have been incorrectly associated with both the absence of work and with the notion that it is an erratic phenomenon that cannot deliberately be encouraged or fostered. In reality it seems very probable that would be poets or other creators, who sit in a corner and wait for the Muse to speak through them without effort on their part, may be doomed to wait in vain!

Associated with the spiritual view of creativity is the notion that any restrictions on children's behavior will crush their creativity. In its strongest form, this view holds that expecting children to be familiar with bodies of facts, or to regulate their behavior in accordance with anybody else's wishes, blocks creativity. However, although excessive dependence on external sources of evaluation, and excessive conformity to social conventions, may well be anticreative, it does not seem likely that creativity is automatically encouraged by the fostering of selfishness, arrogance, contempt for everything but one's own judgment, or by ignorance of the three Rs. Marjoram (1988) explicitly rejected the idea of "freedom" (in the sense of doing whatever you like) as a precondition for creativity in the classroom. His experience suggests that the opposite is the case. Consequently, it is not the purpose of the present book to advise teachers to abdicate all authority, to abandon all established procedures, or to break all rules and regulations. There is a need for reduced emphasis on blind conformity to convention, excessive dependence upon the good opinion of others, and similar attitudes. However, the difference between deemphasizing and abandoning is a substantial one.

Two Uses of the Word *Creativity*

Throughout this book, attention fluctuates between creativity conceptualized as a special kind of thinking or mental functioning (which may be labeled *divergent thinking*), and creativity in the aesthetic/professional sense that people have in mind when they say that Michaelangelo or

Einstein was creative. This fluctuation of meaning is a problem that continually plagues discussions of creativity. As one writer put it, the word is used "with gay abandon" (Nicholls, 1972). When teachers say that they want to encourage creativity, they may have in mind creativity in the Michaelangelo sense. On the other hand, what they actually promote is more likely to be a matter of attitudes, values, emotions, and intellectual skills. The two may not be synonymous: it is not clear, for example, whether possession of certain thinking skills and special attitudes and values actually does lead to real life creativity in the aesthetic/professional sense. Nicholls (1972) discussed the relationship of creativity as a mental ability and actual achievement. Necka (1986) distinguished between "aesthetic," "professional," "artistic," and "scientific" creativity, and Renzulli (1984) pointed out that children may show creativity in different areas at different times.

It would be helpful if some resolution of this uncertainty were achieved, so that teachers understood more clearly whether they were dealing with creativity, with divergent thinking, or with something else. The words are not synonymous and are not equally effective in the emotions they conjure up. For example, it is more impressive and emotionally satisfying, and much more likely to elicit approval from colleagues and parents, for teachers to say that they are concerned about "creativity" rather than "divergent thinking." Some of the confusion between creativity and things like mere self-gratification that has already been referred to probably stems from unduly free use of the emotive word *creativity*.

In this book creativity is conceived of primarily as the capacity to get ideas, especially original, inventive, and novel ideas. To say that children are "creative" means here that they are daring and innovative in their thinking. Suggestions for fostering creativity are not directly aimed at helping them paint paintings, write music, or produce plays (artistic creativity); nor to build novel machines, design new kinds of buildings, or discover hitherto unknown scientific processes (scientific and engineering creativity). Nonetheless, the procedures outlined in later chapters may well have favorable effects in these areas, and there is certainly nothing wrong with setting your sights high. The suggestions in this volume have evolved from concentration on creativity as a special kind of thinking. In addition to intellectual skills, however, the creative way of thinking requires motivation, courage, a sense of recognition, and similar factors. Thus, the discussion of creativity in this book derives from a consideration of its basic psychological processes, both intellectual and affective.

The question of how to foster those psychological processes and states which are favorable to creativity is approached in a broad manner. In particular, it is emphasized that the capacity for daring, inventive, and innovative thinking requires more than merely possession of appropriate intellectual skills (i.e., discussion goes beyond simply the cognitive aspects). Bold, innovative, and free-ranging thinking depends, not only upon the strictly intellectual, but also upon motivational and emotional factors, as has been emphasized in many of the best known psychological studies in the area. A cogent early criticism of the tendency to conceptualize creativity in purely cognitive terms was made by Cattell and Butcher (1968). Nicholls (1972) summarized "classic" studies by Roe, MacKinnon, Taylor, and Barron that emphasized the importance of motivation in creative achievement in real life. More recently, Amabile (1983; Amabile, Goldfarb, & Brackfield, 1990) and Necka (1986) have examined the role of motivation in detail, and Motamedi (1982, p. 84) wrote of the "courage to create." Children will branch out from the conventional in their thinking not only when they possess appropriate mental skills, but when they want to do so, and when they have the confidence to do so. For this reason, the discussion of ways of increasing creative thinking in school children stresses not only enhancement of the ability to get ideas, but also fostering the desire and developing the courage to do so.

Excessive Enthusiasm for Creativity

Extremely loose use of the term *creativity* has contributed to a tendency for parents and teachers to become excessively enthusiastic about it. One result that has already been mentioned is the belief that all behavioral restrictions or expectations should be abandoned. A second effect of "going overboard" for creativity is a tendency to denigrate conventional thinking processes. In fact there are good grounds for believing that such thinking is one of the key intellectual processes, and that it is involved in creative as well as noncreative activities. Bruner (1962) and Schubert (1973) emphasized the role of conventional thinking as a necessary but not sufficient prerequisite for creativity. A recent report on the research of Facaoaru (1985) called for a "two track approach." Thus, teachers who reject any knowledge of factual subject matter are not necessarily helping their students to be creative, nor preparing them for a satisfying later life.

There are many conventional thinking processes that are invaluable for getting along in life and necessary for useful learning. It is difficult to think of a simpler or more effective way of mastering certain basic number combinations than learning tables by heart. It is also difficult to see how a foreign language could be acquired without large amounts of rote learning, especially without living in the foreign country. Consequently, teachers would be advised to avoid adopting, or appearing to adopt, the position that creative thinking is the only kind of thinking that is worthwhile. Attempts to stamp out conventional thinking and force all students to function divergently at all times represent an extremism that does not differ in principle from total failure to recognize the importance of creativity. What is being advocated in this monograph is recognition of alternative modes of intellectual functioning, not the substitution of one tyranny for another.

CREATIVITY AND GIFTEDNESS

The rise of interest in giftedness in the 1980s led to renewed discussion of creativity, which began to be seen as an integral element of giftedness. The result was a new surge of research on creativity. In retrospect, it is apparent that, from the very beginning of the creativity wave of the late 1950s and 1960s, it was seen as an element of high academic achievement. In the United States, the purpose of the initial education act on creativity was production of creative scientists and engineers capable of keeping up with those of the Soviet Union. However, perhaps under the influence of the seminal study of Getzels and Jackson (1962), in which creativity and intelligence were regarded as conflicting or competing mental abilities, research on creativity mainly treated it as a separate ability. Getzels and Jackson identified a group of pupils high on intelligence but low on creativity and a contrasting group high on creativity but low on intelligence, and showed that the high creativity–low intelligence group obtained grades as good as those of the highly intelligent pupils. Nonetheless, it quickly became apparent that some kind of combination of "creativity" and "intelligence" is favorable for school achievement. Wallach and Kogan (1965) extended the work of Getzels and Jackson by looking at children high on both abilities and those low on both. With schoolchildren in Canada (Cropley, 1967a) and university students in Australia (Cropley, 1967b), I showed that, although the highly intelligent–low creative students obtained good marks, they were consistently outstripped by students high on both characteristics. This superiority of achievement among people combining conventional intelligence and creativity became more pronounced as the level of education increased (i.e., from Grade 7 to first year university to final year university to honors level studies). In Sierwald's (1989) longitudinal study in West Germany, pupils of very high intelligence but without corresponding creativity surpassed those merely high on creativity, but in all other cases those higher on creativity achieved better.

In a review of research, Humphreys (1985) confirmed that IQ scores are the best single predictor of academic achievement over the whole range of ability. However, the situation is somewhat different in the case of gifted achievement—indeed, my own study of Australian students just mentioned showed that first class honors students scored high on creativity measures, whereas students with less outstanding results tended to be "merely" intelligent. A study of successful scientists at Cambridge University (Gibson & Light, 1967) showed that many of them had IQs under 130, the traditional cutoff point for identifying giftedness. Bayer and Folger (1966) reported similar findings for the United States. More recently, Facaoaru (1985) showed that Romanian engineers regarded as unusually capable in a demanding practical activity did not differ from the less capable in IQ scores. High achievement depended upon a combination of conventional abilities (good memory, logical thinking, knowledge of facts, accuracy, etc.) and creative abilities (generating ideas, recognizing alternative possibilities, seeing unexpected combinations, having the courage to try the unusual, and so on).

An early but nonetheless very interesting study relating creativity to achievement was that of Hudson (1968). He offered high school graduates seeking admission to the prestigious Cambridge University the opportunity of supplementing the admissions examination by taking an additional test—a test of creativity. Subsequently, 31 students were admitted on the basis of this test, although they had not scored particularly high on the conventional achievement tests. Of these people, 10 scored very high on the creativity test; it is interesting to look in detail at their performance at university. At the end of the first year of the 3-year program, only three of them achieved a grade equivalent to A or B+, and one actually dropped out. After 2 years, five of the remaining nine had B+ or better, and at the end of their program, seven of nine reached this level—the remaining two achieved a B average. Thus, 70% of the creative group (7 out of 10), and in fact 78% (7 out of 9) of those who completed the program, had B+ or better. A proportion of "good" grade point averages this high is normally reached only by a special group of "scholars," selected on the basis of exceptionally high marks on the conventional tests of the entrance exam.

Hassenstein (1988) concluded that a new term is needed for referring to the capacity to deal unusually effectively with the external world, because creativity and intelligence are simply elements of a more comprehensive giftedness. He suggested "Klugheit" (cleverness), a combination of knowledge, accurate observation, good memory and logical thinking (usually regarded as aspects of intelligence), inventiveness, unusual associations, and fantasy (usually seen as aspects of creativity) and inner drive, capacity for being enthused or "turned on," and flexibility (motivational properties of the individual). That "true" giftedness (Cropley, 1981) requires both conventional intelligence and creativity is now widely accepted: according to Matyushkin (1990), psychologists and educators in the Soviet Union see creativity as an integral part of high ability. Mehlhorn, Chalupsky, Kauke, Lorf-Kolker, Mehlhorn, and Paetzold (1988), in reviewing his own and other research on giftedness in the former German Democratic Republic, treated creativity as an indispensable element. A recent North American review of "scientific genius" (Simonton, 1988) made it quite clear that creativity is a central aspect of this phenomenon.

CREATIVITY IN EVERYDAY LIFE

Despite what has just been said, it is not necessary to conceptualize creativity as something for a small group of gifted people. It is important for everyone. Nicholls (1972) was one of the first to make this point explicit in a paper entitled "Creativity in the person who will never produce anything original and useful: The concept of creativity as a normally distributed trait." Richards, Kinney, Bennet and Merzel (1988) particularly emphasized creative activities carried out in everyday life by "ordinary" men and women. At work every day, creativity was divided about equally between the arts, the sciences, the humanities, the social sciences, organizational roles, and leadership. Leisure time creative activities were, however, almost completely confined to the crafts and the fine arts.

If creativity is to be found at all levels of ability and in everyday settings, it is interesting to see how it manifests itself. Several of my students have carried out investigations of creativity in the present sense, and three of these are presented below. All the projects described focus on everyday life. They are all modest in scope and scientific rigor, but close to reality. Schwarzkopf (1981) carried out a longitudinal study with nine adult women who met once a week and worked "creatively" on sewing, knitting, weaving, crocheting, and similar projects. Factors such as making unexpected combinations, trying out new ideas, or seeing the familiar in a new way were emphasized. At the beginning of the year each woman was rated on a number of personality traits by several relatives and close friends who had no knowledge of the project or its intentions. At the end of the year the women were again rated and the more recent scores compared with those from a year earlier. There were significant differences in the ratings for a number of personality dimensions: In their day-to-day life the women showed less anxiety in unfamiliar situations, were more playful, more self-critical, and less cautious. They were judged to be positively motivated by the need to make difficult decisions, be more independent and lively, show more fantasy, be more goal oriented, and show more task persistence.

Herrmann (1987) compared two soccer teams in a league for 10–12-year-old boys. The one team was coached in an authoritarian way, the other "democratically." Emphasis in the latter situation was on taking personal responsibility, spontaneously doing the unexpected, even having fun. The democratically trained boys produced significantly more novel elements in a creativity test, as well as making a significantly larger number of cross relationships. Correlating these scores with data on a personality test,

Herrmann concluded that the democratic training style in the sporting domain had fostered self-confidence and reduced anxiety, and these had generalized to the test domain. He also showed that the democratically trained boys made significantly more humorous responses, and concluded that the democratic football-training style encouraged the expression of aggression in the form of humor rather than violence on the field.

Scheliga (1988) tested a group of dedicated amateur jazz musicians—mainly playing in jazz cellars along the famous (or infamous) Hamburg Reeperbahn—with a paper-and-pencil creativity test. They scored significantly higher than a control group of lab technicians on dimensions such as spontaneity, wealth of ideas, power of association, willingness to take risks, and flexibility. An important conclusion by Scheliga was that "latent" creativity had been "released" by participation in music making, which offers (especially in the form of jazz improvisation) special psychological opportunities: stress on individuality, elimination of inhibitions, encouragement of fantasy, confrontation with one's own emotions, use of nonverbal forms of expression, and the like. Nonetheless, the musician must remain within a particular framework—the product must be relevant to the main musical theme—so that blind unconventionality is not called for.

CREATIVITY AND SCHOOL

Creativity and Educational Equality

A prominent theme in much recent educational writing has been that of equality. In earlier writings, this concept was usually seen as involving the provision to children of different social classes, ethnic backgrounds, and so on, of physical facilities for schooling that were of equal quality, and of teachers who were equally well qualified. Failure to capitalize on such equal opportunities was then seen as the fault of the individuals concerned, because they had been offered what was regarded as an equal chance. However, findings in the United States (Coleman, 1966; Jencks et al., 1972) have indicated that, even where equality of physical plant and faculty have been more nearly achieved than had been thought, pronounced inequalities have persisted in the results of the education process. Inequalities of outcome have not been eliminated. Consequently, recent writings have been marked by a shift towards defining educational equality in terms of equal outcomes, as defined by grades, income as adults, and similar factors, for children from both privileged and underprivileged sectors of society.

The problem of inequality becomes particularly acute when it is borne in mind that, according to recent evidence, children enter school with markedly different patterns of aspirations and values already well established, and that these differences persist despite teachers' efforts (Bloom, 1976). Nonetheless, a strong thrust towards equality in the sense of homogeneity has recently taken hold in educational thinking. It is not enough in the view of many writers to offer equal opportunities for each student to develop along a personal path of self-fulfillment, because those children whose motives, values, and skills do not conform to certain conventional patterns will not obtain high grades in school, or high incomes in the work world. As a result, they will be unequal.

In this climate of opinion, suggesting that children's differences from each other should be emphasized and that diverging patterns of thinking should be encouraged, has a ring of élitism about it. Certainly, fostering creativity in the classroom seems to be a process that would emphasize differences rather than increase homogeneity. However, for some educational thinkers, recent stress on the importance of homogeneity in education seems to imply both a frighteningly authoritarian system of classroom management (how would teachers stamp out persistent idiosyncrasies?) and also a narrow view of equality. Both of these are specifically rejected in the present text. It is argued here that a more promising understanding of equality is to think of it in terms of fulfillment of each particular child's special patterns of hopes, aspirations, and values, rather than of the imposition of a standard pattern, even if this is done with the noblest motives. The former conceptualization offers more interesting prospects (to me at least) as an educational ideal.

It is true, however, that certain patterns of fulfillment currently lead to more substantial monetary rewards in adult life. The answer to this problem may well lie in fostering a society that is willing to tolerate a broader range of personal development and more equal evaluation of differing paths of vocational fulfillment, so that children whose schooling has helped them to develop in an individual way can enter a work world in which a much wider range of jobs offer challenge, adequate income, and acceptable social status. Schools can contribute to the development of such a society by recognizing and encouraging many different ways of thinking (Milgram, 1990). An early study casting doubt on the explanation of educational inequality in the United States purely in terms of differences in financing was that of Coleman (1966). Later, reanalyzing the Coleman data, Jencks et al. (1972) showed the importance of attitudes and values, although his conclusion that the school can scarcely alter these has been shown to be too pessimistic (e.g., Rutter, 1979). In this book I assume that teachers can influence children's knowledge, skills, values, attitudes, and habits. Thus, the basic thrust of the present text is in the opposite direction from that taken by those who advocate equality in the narrow and stifling sense of homogeneity. Ultimately, it is my belief that true equality of a humane kind will be fostered by a recognition of the wide diversity of human psychological functioning, and the development of both schools and societies that are highly tolerant of such diversity.

Taking Creativity Seriously in Schools

Although he was writing at the turn of the present century, and was chiefly concerned with fostering creativity in people of exceptional talent—whereas the present book focuses on all children—the German educator Rein (1904) laid the emphasis in his discussion of the fostering of creativity squarely where it is laid in the present book, on the school. Rein emphasized that neither learning about creativity nor simply being blindly "creative" is enough. What is needed is a classroom which brings out children's creative potentials through a combination of conventional learning and creative activity. I have translated one passage from his writings which seems to me to summarize my position:

> You cannot become a painter, poet or musician merely by reading books on painting, poetry or music. However, simply daubing paint on the canvas, making up doggerel or stringing musical notes together does not make you an artists either. Above all, two things are necessary: creative potential, on the one hand, and schooling which takes creativity seriously, on the other. (Rein, 1904, p. 231)

FURTHER READING

Getzels, J.W., & Jackson, P.W. (1962). *Creativity and intelligence.* New York: Wiley.
Marjoram, T. (1988). *Teaching able children.* London: Kogan Page.
Simonton, D.K. (1988). *Scientific genius. A psychology of science.* Cambridge, UK: Cambridge University Press.
Weisberg, R.W. (1986). *Creativity, genius, and other myths.* New York: Freeman.

2

Creativity, Society, and School

CREATIVITY AND THE CREATIVE PERSON

Identifying Creativity

Educational thinking in recent years has been marked by many shifts of emphasis, not all of them greeted by all teachers with equal enthusiasm. One example is that of creativity. Educational theorists and curriculum planners have exhorted teachers to encourage creativity, because it is thought to be beneficial for the individual, for the society, and for classroom learning. However, creativity has tended to become a catch cry that means all things to all people, and a wide range of behaviors has been justified on the grounds that they are likely to foster creativity. Verbal facility, for example, may be mistaken for creativity, although a child who is merely talkative or even glib is not necessarily being creative. It is important, in fact, to distinguish between children who are truly creative and those who are merely facile, or perhaps it would be better to say between behaviors that are truly creative and those which are simply slick or attention catching. Mere nonconformity, for example, may be mistaken for creativity, although unusual, flamboyant, attention-seeking, or disruptive behaviors are by no means necessarily indicators of creativity. Displaying independence by breaking the rules and by general classroom misbehavior, such as failing to hand in assignments, not keeping schedules, or being untidy, are not intrinsic signs of creativity, even if some genuinely creative people behave this way. Torrance (1963), Bruner (1962), and Lowenfeld (1957) presented early attempts to define some of the key features of truly creative behavior. More recent analyses are those of Taylor (1975) and Necka (1986).

It is true that several writers have emphasized that factors like full personal growth, self-fulfillment, actualization of individual potentials, and similar properties are characteristic of creative people. Among the best known proponents of self-fulfillment and self-actualization as educational goals are Rogers (1961) and Maslow (1954). It is not suggested here that these desirable goals can be neglected, but only that it is possible to debase the notion of creativity by confusing it with self-indulgence. Nonetheless, it remains true that relatively undisciplined and even antisocial behavior is sometimes seen among creative people. As a result, some teachers have tolerated behavior that has seemed to others to be destructive, stupid, or self-indulgent, in the hope that they were helping students to express their creativity. Other teachers have adopted the opposite strategy, rejecting as empty cliché mongering the whole movement towards recognition of children's creative potentials. Consequently, teachers and parents interested in developing creativity in children need to be able to distinguish between creativity and certain behaviors which sometimes accompany it, but which may also have nothing to do with creativity itself. An important distinction was made by Cattell and Butcher (1968) between "genuine" creativity and mere "pseudocreativity." Heinelt (1974) added "quasicreativity," and Hammer (1964), Kneller (1965), and Besemer and Treffinger (1981) distinguished between genuine creativity and mere facileness, slickness, glibness, or unconventionality. Many writers, such as Sappington and Farrar (1982), have emphasized that true creativity must necessarily involve some novel product (even if in the form of an idea) that "conforms to reality constraints" (p. 68). In this text, the emphasis is, nonetheless, frequently upon creativity in the sense of psychological states and processes, not upon end products. A failure to make the distinction just discussed may result in tolerance for behaviors (such as those just outlined) which have no claim to capturing the essence of creativity at all, and may even stem from sheer naughtiness or some other source totally unrelated to creativity.

One aim of this book is to help resolve these kinds of problems by crystallizing for teachers a concept of classroom creativity. It is unreasonable to expect teachers to tolerate disruptive behavior from their pupils through fear of repressing creativity, but it is also disastrous if they inhibit innovative, free-ranging thinking because they regard it as mere misbehavior.

Creativity Facilitating Skills

Creativity facilitating skills have been outlined more fully by Torrance and Hall (1980), Necka (1986), and Sternberg (1985, 1988). Although this list is not necessarily exhaustive, some of the key properties of creative thinking may be described as follows:

> *Sensitivity to Problems*—Creative thinkers show high levels of skill in pinpointing problems. They may see defects in proffered solutions and question the established wisdom given in textbooks.
>
> *Redefinition of Problems*—Creative thinkers are frequently able to restate a problem in new terms which provide a fresh line of approach or new insights.
>
> *Penetration*—Creative thinkers often display a knack for going straight to the heart of a problem, discarding or disregarding irrelevant details.
>
> *Analysis and Synthesis*—Creative thinkers show high levels of ability both to break down a problem into its constituent parts and also to see connections between the elements of a problem and other areas of experience.
>
> *Ideational Fluency*—Having pinpointed, analyzed, and defined the problem, creative thinkers are particularly skillful at generating large numbers of relevant ideas. (Some writers argue that this property is the key intellectual ability involved in creativity.)
>
> *Flexibility*—Creative thinkers show flexibility as well as fluency. This involves their ability to change their line of thinking and switch to a new approach.
>
> *Originality*—Finally, creative thinkers show high levels of ability to generate novel and unusual ideas.

A similar list of cognitive processes was developed by the Polish psychologist Necka (1986):

1. Forming associations;
2. Recognizing similarities;
3. Constructing metaphors;
4. Carrying out transformations;
5. Selectively directing one's own attention;
6. Seeing the abstract aspects of the concrete.

The importance of "metacognition" has also been emphasized (see Sternberg, 1985). (*Metacognitive* processes are those which make it possible to reflect upon one's own cognitions.) Among the most important metacognitive processes in creativity are:

1. Recognizing the nature of the problem;
2. Representing the problem internally;

3. Deciding which of the myriad solution strategies are most promising;
4. Choosing and organizing cognitive resources;
5. Combining thinking strategies to develop new lines of attack;
6. Evaluating the degree of progress achieved by an approach;
7. Identifying new lines of attack when old ones prove to be unfruitful.

Simonton (1988) advanced what he called the "chance-configuration" model of genius; his approach can, however, be applied to creativity. Building on Campbell's (1960) argument that creativity involves blind variation, Simonton concluded—somewhat adapted for present purposes—that creativity involves production of a large number of associations, more or less randomly or blindly, and the chance occurrences of "configurations"—happy combinations which represent just what is needed to solve the problem in question. The creative person is especially good, not only at producing associations, but also at recognizing that a configuration has occurred and grasping that it offers a solution. Weisberg (1986) examined self-reports and case studies of famous creators and combined this information with data obtained in experimental studies. He concluded that creativity arises from "chains" of ideas connected associately in a long series of strictly logical small steps, for which knowledge of the field is vital.

Altshuller (1984) criticized the random variation approach to creativity, arguing that running through all possible configurations in a blind manner would involve too many "empty" trials. Some mechanism is needed for presorting the infinitely large chain of associations which would arise if all possible permutations and combinations were treated as equally deserving; most must be rejected in advance. Sternberg's "metacognitive" approach argues that such mechanisms do exist, and shows what they might be like—rules for distinguishing in advance blind alleys from promising approaches, for choosing between competing lines of attack, for evaluating emerging solutions and deciding the best way to continue, and the like. In China, Zha (1986) showed that gifted children possessed highly effective tactics for searching for information in the memory store. Research in the former German Democratic Republic (Klix & van de Meer, 1986) demonstrated the importance in gifted achievement of, among other factors, "preorganizing" of information.

Characteristics of the Creative Thinker

Apart from special properties of thinking (cognitive processes), creative people display typical personal characteristics. Farisha (1978) concluded that personality is consistently emphasized in research on creativity. Relevant studies include those of Dellas and Gaier (1970), Motamedi

(1982), Runco (1989), and Treffinger, Isaksen, and Firestein (1983). In general, descriptions of the creative personality show a person who is intelligent and capable of sustained hard work, who seeks change and adventure, who is impulsive, and who does not like to conform. The creative thinker is inclined to avoid adherence to strict and restrictive schedules and, as a result, may show a certain disregard for observing rules and details of plans. In fact, many creative individuals give a strong impression of being disorganized, although they may also show meticulous attention to detail when circumstances require it.

Creative individuals are also likely to challenge authority—not only in the intellectual sphere, where scientific or other scholarly authorities are questioned, but also in the social sphere, where established customs and traditions may be challenged. These characteristics of creative people are summarized in the list that follows.

Creative individuals:

- seek change and adventure;
- express impulses and are consequently sometimes undisciplined, although they are perfectly capable of highly disciplined behavior when pursuing a goal which they value;
- readily accept new ideas;
- challenge rules and authorities on occasion;
- dislike conformity and conformists;
- are inclined to be disorganized, but are capable of attention to details when pursuing a valued goal;
- prefer loose and flexible planning;
- are very skillful at "rolling with the punches" and adapting quickly to circumstances; and
- are usually friendly, but may sometimes be withdrawn or else may talk too much.

A particular combination of these traits can lead to apparently badly disorganized and careless behavior, to seeming rebelliousness, or to extreme self-centeredness. For this reason, highly creative children may sometimes be difficult to handle in the classroom. Similarly, they may be regarded as unpredictable, unfriendly, or stupid by peers. This inconsistency and display of socially unacceptable behavior may lead to clashes between creative children and their teachers or their peers.

Research studies have delineated additional traits characteristic of highly creative children. These include, for example, the tendency to set themselves very high goals or have high levels of motivation for achievement. Such children may also be "uneven" in their development, showing precocious ability in some areas and poor achievement in others. An example of this is the child who is exceptionally good at music but shows poor development of sporting skills. These children tend to have strong and well-formed self-images, as a result of which they may appear arrogant to some people. They display high levels of curiosity, which frequently involves them in risk-taking behavior. "Risks" are not necessarily physical risks, but may be intellectual or social in nature. They possess a well-developed sense of humor and may annoy other people by making apparently pointless or irrelevant jokes that are difficult for others to understand. Similarly, they are inclined to produce "way-out" ideas. All of these traits may disturb people with whom they come into contact and even result in rejection by some teachers and children.

CREATIVITY AND CLASSROOM VALUES

What Do Teachers Value?

Unfortunately, the educational literature suggests that the kinds of behavioral and personality traits that commonly characterize creative individuals are not those which teachers prefer in their pupils. Research in a number of different countries indicates that teachers almost universally prefer children who are:

> courteous and considerate of others,
> punctual,
> energetic and industrious;
> popular with their peers;
> "well-rounded,"
> receptive to other people's ideas, and
> obedient.

It is noticeable that properties such as willingness to take risks, or be innovative, bold, flexible, and original, are all marked by their absence from this list. Thus, there are grounds for believing that teachers greatly overvalue behavioral and personal properties that are not normally characteristic of creative pupils.

This impression has been confirmed by studies of the kinds of intellectual activity teachers prefer in their students. Some data obtained in the U.S. are summarized in Table 2.1, which shows the kinds of mental activity preferred by teachers in several different subject areas. Of the science teachers, nearly 95% regarded "conservative" thinking activities (recognition of learned material, memorization, accuracy) as of primary importance. In Social Studies classes, emphasis on this kind of thinking reached

Table 2.1.   Student activities most valued by teachers*

	Student Activity	Percentage of teachers valuing most highly in					
		Science		Social Studies		Language Arts	
	Recognition of learned material	70.7		76.6		24.6	
"Conservative" Activities	Memorization	5.3	94.7%	5.4	98.6%	3.4	85.9%
	Accuracy	18.7		16.5		57.9	
"Innovative" Activities	Independent thinking, constructive criticism, etc.	1.7		0.9		8.8	
			5.3%		1.4%		14.0%
	Critical evaluation, comparative assessment, decision making, etc.	3.6		0.5		5.2	

*This table is based on material from Torrance (1962, 1963).

almost 100%. Even in the case of teachers of Language Arts, no fewer than 86% of teachers' efforts was directed towards fostering accuracy and memory. These figures strongly suggest that inadequate attention is paid to promoting creative thinking in many classrooms. Although they were obtained about 30 years ago, more recent observations suggest that the current situation may be only slightly more favorable (e.g., Howieson, 1984; Obuche, 1986).

The school curriculum is still dominated by "closed content." What children are supposed to learn is specified by other people and is written down in advance in the form of programs, lesson plans, set exercises, and the like. The curriculum is also dominated by "convergent content," with the main emphasis on correct, "best" answers arrived at through the use of strictly logical, even "officially approved" thinking processes. (The discussion of "closed content" and "convergent content" is taken from Bloom, 1971.) Correct answers and the processes for obtaining them are not unimportant, of course. On the contrary, as has already been stressed, there is a major place for them in the classroom. There is no doubt that it is important for children to learn things which are useful or even necessary for their smooth and relatively effortless participation in daily life. The important point in the present context, however, is that, although teachers, administrators, and planners usually pay lip service to divergent thinking or creative processes, school curricula, classroom practice, and evaluation methods are usually dominated by convergent content (Yager, 1989). This may reach the point where, for all practical purposes, teachers do not know how to give due emphasis to divergent content in their day-to-day work or may even lack a framework for conceptualizing the problem just outlined, except perhaps in a vague and general way. It is to be hoped that the present text will help to provide such a framework.

Good examples of the effects of excessive emphasis on closed or convergent content are to be seen in two practical experiences I recall. In an oral examination I asked a candidate what he understood under the term *age*. He replied that age is defined by the amount of time which has passed between an individual's birth and the present moment. Because the exam in question was in psychology, I asked him if he could make some suggestions off the top of his head about the elements of a psychological definition of age. He replied that the concept *age* already existed with a set meaning (he had just given it), and that speculating in the way I had invited would be a very dangerous matter, for it would mean that we could never be sure what an expression meant. Several years ago I asked a 14-year-old schoolgirl if she could offer a few suggestions about the consequences which would follow if the clouds suddenly had strings hanging down from them. She replied that it was impossible for her to imagine such a situation, because she knew that clouds are only water vapor and water vapor could not support the weight of strings long enough to reach down to the earth. When I asked her to use her imagination and pretend that such strings really existed, she replied that she could not imagine something which she knew to be impossible. Although it is clear that the answers given by both the students were strictly correct and even in a certain sense admirable, I myself (and I believe many readers) have the feeling that something is lacking in the students' reactions to the invitations to speculate, imagine, or fantasize. Despite the fact that both were highly intelligent young people (the girl achieved an IQ of 140), their application of intelligence to the questions just outlined left something to be desired.

Age-Related "Troughs" in Creativity

Schools and society in general do not encourage creative thinking in students to the extent that they might. One result of this is the occurrence of "troughs" in the level of creative thinking displayed by schoolchildren. Research in several countries has shown that there is a steady improvement in children's capacity to think creatively from kindergarten to the end of grade 3. However, a sharp drop ensues in grade 4; growth occurs again in grades 4, 5, and 6, but there is a second sharp drop in grade 7. Finally, there is slow growth during the high school years. An early discussion of "troughs" in creativity at different ages is to be found in Torrance (1963). More recently, Krampen, Freilinger, and Wilmes (1988), and Smith and

Carlsson (1989), reported that such troughs really do exist: they occur at about 6 years and at a point between 10 and 16 years, depending upon the individual and the society.

Reasons for this pattern of peaks and troughs in creative thinking are probably very complex. At about the grade 3 level most children develop a new understanding of the world about them, of cause and effect relationships, and of abstract concepts. Similarly, at about grade 6 further growth takes place, with greatly increased ability to handle abstract ideas and to formulate and test hypotheses. Piaget (e.g., Inhelder & Piaget, 1958) and Bruner (e.g., 1972) carried out relevant empirical investigations of the development of thinking. This process of "changing into a higher gear" might reasonably be expected to impede creative thinking. A study in Australia even concluded that the "drop" is actually an artifact of changes in testing procedures and has little at all to do with psychological development.

Despite this, there are grounds for believing that the creativity slump may be related to peer pressures, as a result of the transition from infant school to primary school in the first instance, and primary to secondary school in the second. In addition, changed teacher expectations in about grade 4 and grade 7 may well inhibit creativity. These two points are key transitional stages in school organization, development of peer relations, and advances in children's understanding of the nature of the external world. They may thus be points at which classroom blocks to creativity may assume particular importance.

THE NEED FOR CREATIVITY

Society's Need for Creativity

Teachers widely accept that accuracy and memory are two of the most important kinds of intellectual functioning, and often pay only lip service to divergent thinking processes. Why then has creativity received increased interest recently?

Widespread recognition of the value of creativity in the classroom followed the successful launching by the Russians of the first artificial satellite—Sputnik I. At this time, a massive reappraisal of educational practice occurred in the U.S. After extensive soul searching it was concluded that sheer quantity of trained personnel alone could not guarantee rapid advancement in technology. On the contrary, merely competent and well-trained scientists and engineers reach their limits quickly. The value of a single highly innovative and original thinker (a creative individual) was then recognized, and a great surge of interest in furthering creativity ensued. Many educators concluded that a society which was to survive in the face of rapid scientific and technological advance desperately needed creative thinkers. Guilford (1962), Taylor and Barron (1963), and Yager (1989) discussed the relationship between technological and scientific advancement and creativity, and Toynbee (1962) argued that creativity is crucial in these areas.

A second and related recognition of the value to society of creative thinkers developed at about this time. With the advance of technology, human beings found that many functions which they had previously regarded as their own were being taken over by machines, notably by computers; even computer poetry and computer music began to be publicized. The power and speed of the computer as a calculating machine also became apparent, and human abilities in these areas began to pale into insignificance. In this context it became increasingly clear that the typically human aspects of intelligence were not the reproductive or conservative elements at all. People's dignity and special human characteristics were seen to involve the innovative areas which machines could not enter—the domain of creativity. Creativity provides a means of fostering human dignity in a computer-dominated age in which mere routine thinking is increasingly becoming the domain of the machine (Bruner, 1962).

Finally, in recent years, it has become apparent that a major feature of life is rapid change. It seems likely that the jobs which will be filled by many of today's schoolchildren do not presently exist. In the same way, the personal and social pressures they will face, and the roles in society that they will fill, are presently unknown. Schools are not capable of providing all students with a ready-made set of practical skills which they will be able to apply for the rest of their lives. This is because the skills needed for the future may not be known at present. Knowledge needs to be seen as innovative and adaptive, not fixed and immutable (Langer, Hatem, Joss, & Howell, 1989). Above all, today's children need to be equipped by their schooling with skill at adapting to change. Society's need is for inventive, flexible, and adaptable adults. In view of this need, the capacity of school to develop creative thinking assumes great importance (see Cropley, 1974, for a more detailed discussion).

The Individual's Need for Creativity

One danger arising from these social factors is that individuality will be submerged in the swelling numbers of people now living on the face of the earth, in the increasing complexity of social systems, and in the increasing role of government in such aspects of life as recreation and sport, which were once the domain of the individual. People may be further overwhelmed and confused by the growth of technological means of production, and by uncertainty about which skills will be vocationally relevant in the future. It may well be that the not-too-distant future will see a society in which concrete results of the individual person's efforts will be almost invisible. Individual decisions and individual efforts may shortly have very little effect on things like the extent to which physical comforts such as housing and food are enjoyed. It is even possible that work may cease to be a major determinant of the kind of life a person experiences. In short, the increasing estrangement of individual people from the results of their labors may soon be so far advanced that they come to depend almost entirely on abstract, internal standards to obtain personal satisfactions and a sense of achievement. In such a setting, individuals who are able to shift ambitions, to find satisfaction in achieving personally defined goals, and to respond to challenges arising from within themselves will live the fullest and most satisfying lives.

Mental Health and Creativity

Research has shown that creative thinkers are inclined to be flexible, adventurous, tolerant, and open-minded. They are also curious and willing to allow themselves a wide range of experiences, and have the ability to reject or revise earlier attitudes and opinions relatively easily. They tend to have a strong self-image, so that they are confident about who they are and where they are going. In situations of conflict, they are able to hold their ground without self-doubts and misgivings, but to revise their views when it is appropriate to do so. This means that they tend to be self-assured and confident in social relations. By contrast, persons in whom creative behavior is suppressed have been described as possessing uncertain and poorly formed self-concepts. In situations where strongly adhered-to values or beliefs are challenged, they experience difficulty in revising their views. A shift of ground represents a challenge to an already weak and uncertain self-concept. As a result, they display fearful behavior in conflict situations and may suffer continual neurotic conflicts marked by self-doubts and uncertainty. Frequently, in children, these kinds of problem tend to be externalized and to manifest themselves in aggressive, violent, or self-destructive behavior. It is thus apparent that the creative thinker is in a state conducive to favorable mental health (Cropley, 1990; Rothenberg, 1990). On the other hand, the person in whom such thinking is strictly suppressed is in a "sensitive" position, in which challenge, conflict, and uncertainty can quickly lead, not to personal growth, but to mental ill health.

The idea that there is a relationship between creativity and mental health is one of psychology's oldest issues. Plato, for instance, concluded that poets are set aside from ordinary mortals by the fact that the gods speak through them. More than 2,000 years later, at the beginning of the era of modern psychology, Lombroso (1891) argued that genius and madness are closely allied. Over the years, this theme has repeatedly been the subject of research (e.g., Ellis, 1926; Juda, 1949; McNeil, 1971; Rothenberg, 1983). The idea of a connection between creativity and mental illness has received renewed attention in the last few years, and sufficient data have been accumulated to permit a number of general conclusions. Broadly speaking, two approaches are to be seen: Some studies examine highly creative individuals and ask whether they display a significantly higher incidence of mental illness than ordinary members of the public (e.g., Andreasen, 1987; Holden, 1987). Others study people regarded as "odd" (Weeks & Ward, 1988) or as mentally ill (e.g., Richards, Kinney, Lunde, Bennet, & Merzel, 1988) and ask whether they are unusually creative.

In seeking to explain the psychological connection between creativity and mental illness, Cropley and Sikand (1973) initially adopted a cognitive position, hypothesizing that it lies in the area of thinking and related processes. They showed that the members of a group of creative architects, writers, musicians, and the like resembled a sample of patients diagnosed as schizophrenic in some aspects of the cognitive domain, and that both groups were significantly different from "normals" (people who were neither creative nor schizophrenic). However, they also found that, despite the cognitive similarities between schizophrenics and creatives, there were substantial noncognitive differences: The creative individuals tended to be excited by unusual associations in their own thinking and tried to build upon them, whereas the schizophrenics were frightened by them and tried to avoid them. Thus, Cropley and Sikand concluded that the relationship between creativity and psychological disturbance is more a matter of affect than of different ways of thinking.

Jamison (1989) studied 47 British artists and writers who had all either won major awards or were members of the Royal Academy. She found that 18 had been treated for maniac-depressive conditions, a figure six times as high as would be expected in the general populace. Linking these data with observations of famous creative people from the past such as Byron, Shelley, Coleridge, and Poe—who were apparently able to work creatively only when their mood was elevated—Jamison concluded that mood "highs" are essential for creativity. Such "highs" are characterized by unusual fluency in thinking (i.e., cognitive processes), but also by high levels of motivation and an overwhelming feeling of self-confidence (affective variables). However, as both Holden and Andreasen emphasized, the connection between affective disorders and creativity may not be directly causal in nature at all: It is possible that wide mood swings, on the one hand, and rich imagination and high motivation to create, on the other, both result from a common cause without actually influencing one another directly. Such a common cause could be "emotional reactivity" (Holden) or possession of a particularly labile or "fine-tuned" (Andreason) nervous system)— a tendency to react unusually strongly to external stimuli and internal mood signals. It is important to notice that, as Richards et al. (1988) concluded after examining the results of a number of studies in the area, florid psychosis does not seem to be a favorable condition for creative productivity; nonetheless, mild affective disorders may favor it, possibly through mechanisms such as those just outlined (also see Richards & Kinney, 1990).

As has been shown in research already mentioned, creativity is connected with personal properties such as flexibility, openness, autonomy, humor, playfulness, willingness to try things, perseverance, "stickability," elaboration of ideas, realistic self-assessment, and similar characteristics. Generally, these properties have been ascertained in studies of highly creative people, and they are usually thought of as prerequisites for the emergence of creativity (i.e., as something out of which creativity arises, or whose absence makes creativity impossible). However, theory and research on normal personal development—with or without direct reference to creativity—also emphasize similar properties as core elements of the healthy personality. According to psychoanalytic theory, for instance, the ability to express drives and impulses without excessive use of defense mechanisms, or to admit primary process material into consciousness, for example in the form of humor, requires high ego strength; Ammon (1974) saw creativity as an ego function in itself. According to Hartmann (1958), ego autonomy permits freedom from blind obedience to instinct and from dependence on immediate environmental events; high levels of autonomy make it possible for the individual to cope in a positive way with change, even with catastrophies in life. Anthony (1987) concluded that there is a cause-and-effect relationship between creativity and mental health by arguing that, because creativity is related to ego autonomy, and ego autonomy promotes the capacity to deal with life situations, creativity favors the development of resistance to psychopathology.

In humanistic psychology concepts such as *self* and *self-actualization* are at the heart of healthy personality development. Maslow (1954, 1971) and Rogers (1961), in their classical studies, emphasized the importance of openness, flexibility, and tolerance in the healthy personality. Krystal (1988) made the link between mental health and creativity even more specific in a study in which he also took the unusual step of studying extremely uncreative people. He found that they had considerable difficulties in the area of self: "self-caring" was difficult for them, for instance, while they lacked "self-coherence." Fostering creativity in these people would promote their mental health in the sense of self-realization.

Learning Advantages for the Individual

A valuable distinction in discussing creativity is that between *content learning* (learning of selected facts that are chosen because they are judged by curriculum planners to be useful or necessary) and *process learning* (learning that increases the ability of students to deal effectively with their present and futures lives, especially by increasing their ability to handle novelty). This latter kind of learning may, of course, go on either in or out of school. However, according to Biggs (1973), in the school setting a curriculum oriented towards the fostering of creativity would include skills in:

> locating information,
> turning information into knowledge,
> using highly generalized thinking skills,
> setting one's own objectives, and
> evaluating the outcomes of one's own work.

Early studies—including Cropley (1967a), Moore (1961), Ornstein (1961), and Torrance (1964)—discussed the practical value of creative thinking in the classroom, and Schubert (1975) showed that creative students had higher than average grades and failed less frequently. Possession of such skills yields a number of concrete and practical advantages. Well-developed creative-thinking capacities generate a more effective, broader, more encompassing intellect that can be brought to bear on classroom learning problems. The result has been shown to be superior learning. Furthermore, the effects of creativity are not confined to the intellectual aspects of learning. For example, children who think creatively in the classroom are more likely to find learning intrinsically motivating, pursuing it with vigor and determination. As a result, development of divergent thinking abilities improves attitudes towards learning and fosters motivation for learning.

CAN CREATIVITY BE TAUGHT?

The Components of Creativity

Most discussions of creativity emphasize the importance of innovative, free-ranging thinking. Yet artistic, scientific, and technological creativity involve considerably more than the capacity to think in a divergent or innovative fashion. Research has shown that one of the first essentials for productive creativity in the da Vinci or Einstein sense is *thorough knowledge of the field* (for a recent discussion see Necka, 1986, and Facaoaru, 1985). As a painter, da Vinci was skilled in the craftmanship of his profession. Einstein was thoroughly conversant with the facts of mathematics. Some people recognized as creative have denied the importance of knowledge: for example, Poincarè and A. E. Houseman both attributed their creative work to inspiration. Nonetheless, these writers seem to have been influenced by popular stereotypes concerning the inspirational origins of creativity. Their descriptions of their work prior to the moment of inspiration suggest that, far from coming like a bolt out of the blue, these moments were merely the culmination of a long process of hard work. Gogol stated bluntly that any creator who believes that creativity is mainly inspiration is wrong. Thus, one element of creativity is knowledge of the field, obtained largely through the application of conventional learning skills. Pasteur summarized this point of view by saying, "Chance favors the prepared mind."

Although a particular person may show high levels of conventional thinking skill, exceptional creative-thinking capacity, and high motivation, there seems to be a second important component—that of *talent*. It has been variously conceptualized, but it seems to involve particular and almost unique combinations of sensory, motor, and intellectual capacities that cause a few individuals to display exceptional skill in some quite narrow range of activities, such as in the distinction of musical tones from each other, the recognition of visual patterns, the application of motor and spatial skills, or the grasping and reshaping of ideas.

A third major component of creativity is the *expenditure of great effort* in reaching the end product. Again, Poincarè and Houseman serve as useful examples. Both worked intensively for many years on the problems in which they eventually achieved recognition, Poincarè as a mathematician, Houseman as a poet. Descriptions of D.H. Lawrence's work on his novels indicate that he polished his manuscripts again and again. Indeed, most accounts of the life and work of recognized creative people emphasize their extremely high levels of motivation. Associated with this drive is a belief in oneself—what might be called "expectation of mastery." The combination of high motivation and conviction that success will eventually come often leads to what has been called "hunger" (Stanley, 1984) for experience, or "obsession" with an idea or task. As Edison put it: "Genius is 1% inspiration, 99% perspiration!" According to Renzulli (e.g., 1984), "task commitment" is one of the key defining characteristics of creative people, and Biermann (1985), adopting a historical perspective, emphasized the role "stubbornness" played in the creative achievements of mathematicians in the 17th to 19th centuries.

Summarizing what has just been proposed, it seems that the emergence of creativity depends upon three psychological components: familiarity with a field allied to special talents or abilities, creativity related abilities or

Table 2.2   The three component model of practical creativity[1]

Component	Examples of contents	Possibility of classroom facilitation
1. "Expertise"	Special talents or abilities Thorough knowledge of a content area, special skills	Low High
2. Creativity-related abilities and skills	Ability to concentrate Special thinking skills (e.g., divergent thinking)	Intermediate Theoretically high*
3. Personal characteristics	Task commitment and courage Intrinsic motivation "Expectation of mastery"	All theoretically high*

*Although these elements are theoretically amenable to training, they run counter to the existing school tradition, so that their facilitation is more difficult in practice than might be expected.

[1]This table is reprinted with permission from McLeod & Cropley, *Fostering academic excellence*, Copyright 1989, Pergamon Press PLC.

skills, and appropriate personal properties—these elements are summarized in Table 2.2, which is largely based on ideas in Necka (1986). Knowledge and talent combined with motivation but unaccompanied by creative skills lead to technical achievements whose value should not be ignored, although the spark of creativity is missing. Expertise and creative properties without motivation lead to "abandoned" creativity, and motivation and creativity without expertise yield "infantile" creativity.

A fourth component is also important—especially for this book—even though it is often overlooked. This is the element of *opportunity*. It is possible that many potential creative geniuses may have gone unnoticed because of the absence of this element. The combinations of events which led to the emergence of Michaelangelo is a case in point. His father was a stonemason, and so he had early opportunities to use the tools of the stonemason's trade. As a child he had the good fortune that a local noble recognized his talent. The nobleman became interested in the boy, encouraged his development, and the result was Michaelangelo. As Gallagher (1986) pointed out, we cannot simply sit back and assume that potential will realize itself without any help. This is where the role of school becomes apparent: for many children—especially those whose homes offer little encouragement—it is the major source of opportunity.

Teaching to Develop Creativity

It is thus apparent that creativity is a complex of many factors. It involves attitudes, values, goals, and motivation, as well as special thinking skills, appropriate knowledge, and finally, talent and opportunity. These components can, at least to some extent, be influenced by schools (Langer et al., 1989; Graham, Sawyers, & Debord, 1989; Yager, 1989). Teachers can offer opportunities for the emergence of creativity in a number of ways: they can help students to produce ideas of an inventive and original kind; they can develop classrooms rich in opportunities for the emergence of creativity, and be willing to tolerate creative behavior; they can build up pupils' interest in creativity and convince them of their own potential for being creative.

Teachers may be setting their sights too high if they aim at promoting aesthetic/professional creativity in all students. However, it does lie within their power to promote individual thinking, reward novel solutions to problems, encourage extension of thinking into "illogical" areas, and praise the recognition of previously unseen relationships. They can also emphasize properties like the finding of principles which unite segments of knowledge usually regarded as separate, encourage the reexamination of facts, and inspire the use of imagination. Finally, teachers can stimulate creativity in the classroom through the kinds of model they display in their own attitudes and behavior.

A number of empirical studies have shown that students' disposition to carry on divergent thinking can be fostered by appropriate teacher behaviors. It has also been shown that scores on creativity tests increase after appropriate training. This increase is sometimes persistent, and does not necessarily disappear after a day or two—improvements in creative thinking resulting from training in brainstorming were still observable as much as 4 years later. When physics was taught by inquiry methods in which the teachers restricted themselves to answering "Yes" or "No" to questions posed by pupils, acquisition of knowledge about physics was as good in the case of children taught by the conventional provision of facts by the teacher (see Langer et al., 1989; Suchman, 1961; and Yager, 1989). However, the inquiry-trained students were markedly superior on tests of curiosity and inquisitiveness. They were also observed to be more highly motivated to learn than those taught by conventional methods, and to display greater intrinsic motivation. It has also been shown that children can be taught to produce large numbers of ideas in a relatively short time, and that they can be taught to distinguish between merely numerous ideas and clever, interesting and unusual ones. Covington (1967) went so far as to take the view, not only that creative thinking can be taught, but that it should be the heart of classroom practice, particular disciplines merely offering sets of material to which creative thinking can be applied.

Despite all this, studies of the effects of formal programs aimed at developing a general disposition to be creative have not been encouraging (Mansfield, Busse, & Krepelka, 1978; Rump, 1979). It has been shown that gains in "creativity" occur mainly in activities resembling those in the training procedures, and effects may also be shortlived. Thus, it is an illusion to imagine that teachers can create large numbers of little Michaelangelos, Shakespeares, or Edisons by the application of special teaching methods. Creative genius at such levels requires, among other things, extraordinary talents, which may largely be inborn. Nonetheless, the idea of trying to promote creativity in the classroom by fostering the acquisition of expertise, encouraging creative skills and abilities, and fostering the emergence of appropriate personal properties is not foolish. What is needed is the infusion of day-to-day classroom work with attitudes and values, work habits, teaching and learning methods, and forms of evaluation which are favorable for the getting of ideas, branching out, and trying the new. These properties can play a valuable role in the everyday lives of "ordinary people."

A Classroom Example

A study of the effects of teaching to foster divergent thinking was carried out by Cropley and Feuring (1971) with a group of grade-1 children averaging 6 years and 8 months in age. Their scores on a creativity test were assessed before the commencement of the special teaching. They were then divided into four groups. Two received training in creative thinking, while the other two spent equivalent amounts of time listening to stories read by the teacher. The creativity training involved one 20-minute class session a day for 4 days, which was spent in teaching the children principles for changing things. Each day, a plain white card was held up in front of the class, followed by a card which had been changed, say by drawing a square on it (adding something to it), by making it smaller (changing the size), or by changing its color. An aluminum card was used one day, to demonstrate changing the material, a round card to illustrate changing shape, and cards with pictures of a light bulb, a bell, and a flower to illustrate giving sensory appeal for eye, ear, and nose.

After being shown the principles of change for that day, the children were asked to suggest ideas for changing a particular toy to make it more fun to play with (say, a toy elephant). Half the children were encouraged during the session to tell the teacher as many ideas as they could think of for improving the toy. The other half were urged to offer only interesting and unusual suggestions. Thus, among the children receiving teaching to foster production of ideas, one group was encouraged to produce ideas of high quality, the other to produce merely ideas, regardless of quality. Subsequent to the training, the children were again given a divergent thinking test, and the scores of those who had received special teaching were compared with those who had not. Results indicated that there was a significant improvement in the ability of the trained children to produce unusual ideas. There was no increase in their ability to produce mere numbers of ideas. Training, in fact, affected uncommonness and flexibility of ideas, but not sheer quantity.

These results, and similar findings obtained by a number of researchers in different countries and with children of differing age levels, all suggest that certain kinds of classroom activity can encourage children both to produce ideas for themselves, rather than merely to reproduce ideas that they have previously obtained from the teacher, and also to increase the proportion of creative ideas among those that they develop. Recall also that it has already been argued that fostering such abilities promotes motivation for learning, develops enjoyment of learning, and results in superior learning.

The Interaction of Intellect, Motivation, and Emotion

Creativity, in the sense of innovative, daring, free-ranging, and original thinking has three components. These include the *intellectual* aspect (the power to get ideas), the *motivational* aspect (the willingness to work at getting ideas and communicating them when they have been obtained), and the *emotional* aspect (the courage to think in "different" ways, to resist pressure to conform, to risk ridicule, and so on). All three elements need to be developed if children are to think creatively, for creativity results from their interaction with each other.

As will be shown in Chapters 3 and 4, society in general and educators in particular have not always valued traits that are favorable to creative thinking. Intelligence has been understood in a restricted sense, and society and peer groups have presented "blocks" to the production and communication of novel ideas. The balance of the book discusses some of these blocks, and then outlines ways in which teachers can overcome them. The goal is to foster the ability to get ideas, to build motivation, and to develop emotional climates in the classroom in which creative thinking will freely occur.

CASE STUDIES

One purpose of this book was to emphasize real-life experiences teachers and students have had in actual classrooms. In pursuing this purpose, people were asked to write down episodes from their own school lives that illustrated some of the points raised in various parts of the book. Several of the anecdotes have been selected, and have been included at the end of each chapter under the heading "Case Studies." They provide illustrations of some of the various principles spelled out in each chapter as they have occurred in real classrooms. The behaviors referred to in the case studies are not necessarily examples of creativity in themselves. Some of them involve conventional behavior which provided the occasion for creativity fostering or inhibiting actions on the part of teachers. Each of these case studies describes some classroom situation as a real student saw it. The words are those of the students themselves.

> *Fostering and rewarding imaginative behavior*—In a high school level class in which the general method of teaching courses in English was to "read and discuss," our class continually bartered for class time to produce a play in the process of being written by a few and to be put on by all. Never thinking that we would indeed get a positive response, our imaginations went at high speed. However, time out of class was granted on condition that the resultant play be taped (sound), and presented as a slide documentary at an annual event. The unorthodox content (at that time) was not what we had expected to be approved, but once it was, work output increased greatly just because someone other than us wanted to see the end result.

Why is this an example of "good" classroom management? Analyze the nature of the teacher's success in the case study.

> *A classroom lacking in creative atmosphere*—I had one teacher in elementary school for years who taught Music, Art, and Fear! The latter was an extra he instilled through a liberal sprinkling of temper tantrums, rapping students over heads with yardsticks, etc. By the end of each session, all of us were invariably uptight for no specific reason other than that, deep within us, we knew we weren't perfect and one day he'd find out our particular weak spots. Generally, we hoped that those with the ill-fated luck of already having displeased him would continue to do so. Didn't learn much in that class about Art and Music, though.

In this classroom, motivation was to avoid being exposed to ridicule or contempt. Interpersonal relations among the students had deteriorated to the point where they heaved sighs of relief if someone else became the teacher's victim, for it meant that they themselves would be spared. A general atmosphere of fear and mistrust had developed, along with self-doubt and uncertainty. What was the special nature of this teacher's failure to establish a classroom open to creativity?

> *Developing a classroom open to inquiry*—A teacher in an introductory German class of 12- and 13-year-olds is explaining the plural forms of the definite article. The children are already familiar with the singular forms, of which there are three—*der, die,* and *das.* In order to encourage the students, the teacher emphasizes that the plural requires much less learning of new

article forms than did the singular. He points out that there is only one form of the definite article in the plural, instead of three, and then goes on: "Not only that, but you don't have to learn any indefinite articles in the plural! What are the indefinite articles again?" A child tells him that they are *ein, eine,* and *ein.* "Good. Those words correspond to the English words *a* or *an.* It's obvious why there's no plural of them, isn't it? There can't possibly be a plural of *a dog* or *an apple,* can there? The word *a* or *an* tells you that there is only one of them, and you can't have more than one of *a dog,* can you?" Most of the children nod or mumble agreement. However, one girl shoots up her hand eagerly: "Mr. Thomas, wouldn't the plural of *a* be *some*? It's indefinite and it's more than one, so it must be plural."

Mr. Thomas appears to fly into a rage. He bursts out: "You stupid child. Can't you keep your mouth shut when I'm trying to explain something? How many times do I have to tell you to pay attention, anyway? Just keep your mind on what we are doing, will you! We don't need any clever little misses here to ask stupid questions. If I have any more trouble out of you, young lady, you'll be sorry!" (The girl waited a long time before asking another "stupid" question.)

The interruption was totally unexpected. Mr. Thomas had only mentioned the indefinite articles to create the impression that the plural forms are easy. He wanted to raise his pupils' flagging spirits. Consideration of indefinite plural forms in German raises a number of problems (such as the need for a special declension of adjectives) which are far too advanced for a class like this one. The teacher wanted to go through the plural forms of the definite article, give his students some practice in using them, and assign the task of learning them by heart for homework. The last thing he wanted was a discussion of other grammatical issues.

Is a teacher who responds in this manner necessarily evil, stupid, or malicious? Try answering this question, and those listed below, relying on the material presented in this monograph. What factors might cause even a well-intentioned and progressive teacher to respond in this way? What kinds of consequences could the teacher's reply to the girl have on classroom atmosphere, both in the long and short term? Recall here what was presented about opening and blocking responses. Imagine that you are the teacher concerned. Try to put yourself in his place. Without actually spending several lessons teaching the relevant grammar, how could you respond in a way which would foster a creativity facilitating classroom atmosphere?

Rewarding novel insights—A grade 3 teacher is introducing her arithmetic class to the topic of division. She explains: "You see, we have to find out how many times the number we are dividing by fits into the other number. How many 2s go to make up the number 4, for example?" A child answers correctly after some urging. "That's right, there are two lots of 2 in the number 4, aren't there? Now how many 2s would there be in 6?" After getting the correct answer, she writes on the blackboard a number 2, then another underneath it, and a third below that. "See, when these three 2s are put together, they make up six. There are three 2s in 6. What we are doing is finding out how many times one number goes into another one. That's called dividing." At this point, the incident of interest for our purposes occurs. One little boy puts up his hand. When the teacher asks him what he wants, he says: Dividing is really like taking away, then, isn't it?"

The child noticed that the teacher reconstructed six from three 2s by adding them together. He realized that breaking down the 6 into its component parts (three 2s, for example) was the opposite process to putting it back together again. Consequently, if three 2s can be made into a six by adding them, a 6 can be made into three 2s by subtracting. In a sense, the child is correct. Division and subtraction are related processes. Older adding machines actually carry out division by a process of successive subtractions. The relatedness of division to subtraction can also be seen in logarithms and in numbers expressed in power notation.

The boy had looked at the familiar problem of division from a novel and unexpected point of view (for grade-3 children). He had seen a relationship not usually emphasized at this level of mathematical sophistication (the relatedness of division to subtraction). What should the teacher do? How would you handle the situation, if you were the teacher? How could you use what we know about creativity? What aspects of the child's behavior are important within the terms of reference emphasized in Chapter 1? How could you, as a teacher, foster those behaviors and encourage their future reappearance, both in this particular boy and also in the class as whole? What kinds of teacher response, both verbal and nonverbal, would most quickly and convincingly foster continued innovative and daring thinking and question asking? How would you advise a colleague who told you about the incident and asked for advice?

FURTHER READING

Albert, R.S. (Ed.). (1983). *Genius and eminence: The social psychology of creativity and exceptional achievement*. Elmsford, NY: Pergamon.

Amabile, T.M. (1983). *The social psychology of creativity*. New York: Springer.

Barron, F.X. (1969). *Creative person and creative process*. New York: Holt, Rinehart & Winston.

Gilchrist, M. (1972). *The psychology of creativity*. Carlton, Australia: Melbourne University Press.

McLeod, J., & Cropley, A.J. (1989). *Fostering academic excellence*. Oxford, UK: Pergamon.

Sternberg, R.J. (Ed.). (1988). *The nature of creativity*. Cambridge, UK: Cambridge University Press.

3

Two Contrasting Concepts of Intellectual Ability

ONE-SIDED UNDERSTANDING OF INTELLECT

Popular acceptance of the notion that certain kinds of differences between people can be explained by the concept of *intelligence*" is relatively new. It is only in recent years that the term has passed into everyday language, and only about 140 years since the existence of differences in what is now called intelligence gained formal, "scientific" recognition. At first, intelligence tests concentrated on measures such as pitch discrimination and visual acuity. However, excessive emphasis on sensorimotor functions was strongly criticized by the French psychologist Binet, who argued that differences between people in mental functioning ought to be studied by observing individuals actually carrying out "mental" tasks. He then published a set of tests of mental functioning based on his view that intelligence involves central or intellectual processes rather than sensory or motor ones.

The scales which Binet devised and the method of scoring that he worked out were, in fact, the first tests of intelligence in the modern sense of the term. They emphasized mental activities more like what nonspecialists have in mind when they talk about intelligence: imagination, attention, comprehension, aesthetic appreciation, persistence, possession of moral values, motor skill, and judgment of visual space. Binet carefully attempted to validate his scales by comparing the scores they yielded with teachers' ratings of children's abilities, and with school marks. He retained tasks which distinguished between high and low achievers and showed good discrimination between children of differing ages. In other words, a particular task was only retained in Binet's test battery if it was relatively easy for children who did well in school and relatively difficult for those who did poorly. In addition, it was necessary that the task became easier and easier for children as their age increased. Thus, the different items of the Binet intelligence test were largely selected on the basis of their ability to predict success in schools as they existed at that time.

The Terman Studies

Although he was not the only American to be heavily influenced by European psychology in the years before and after the turn of the present century, Lewis Terman was the one most responsible for the importing and popularization in the United States of the—at that time—new and revolutionary concept of intelligence. In addition to developing the Stanford Binet intelligence scale, which even today is one of the most important such tests, he further refined techniques for stating the level of intelligence in a numerical form (the intelligence quotient). More important for present purposes, he showed in a famous longitudinal study—the *Genetic studies of genius*—what possession of high ability in the Binet sense meant in real-life terms such as success in school, on the job, and even in marriage. Stated briefly, he and his fellow researchers identified a group of exceptionally able school children, essentially on the basis of IQ scores in the modern sense, and followed the fortunes of these people for the rest of their lives. (The initial publication in the study appeared in 1923. The project is still running, despite the fact that Terman himself is no longer alive.)

As would be expected, the gifted group attained higher than average occupational status. Nearly half were graduates, and scarcely 7% became blue collar workers. When a comparison was made between the 150 members of the gifted group who had been judged to have been the most successful (the A group) and the 150 judged to have been least successful (the C group), several interesting findings emerged. Parental encouragement had been significantly higher for the A group, 96.5% of them having received parental encouragement to attend college, compared with 62.3% of the C group; 15.1% of the A group's parents had "demanded high marks," three times the number of C group parents. The number of C group gifted who reported that they were making satisfactory adjustment had steadily declined over the years. In 1922, 82% had replied positively to this question, but by 1960 this had declined to 46% (compared with 81% for the A group). Whereas only 16% of the A group who had been married were divorced by 1960, 41.5% of the C group had suffered broken marriages.

Terman's subjects had greater than usual interest in science, history, biography, travel, and informational fiction, but less in adventure or mystery fiction. They were not characterized by "all work and no play," the "play information quotient" of the gifted group being 136. The group was as a whole also superior on tests of honesty, trustworthiness, and similar moral traits. Many of the members had been accelerated in school (i.e., had skipped grades), and this practice was not found to have been harmful.

The majority of the gifted children had shown early evidence of superiority, the most commonly reported indications being intellectual curiosity, possession of a wealth of miscellaneous information, and a desire to learn to read. In school, their favorite subjects were those which unselected children found to be the most difficult, and in the quantity and quality of their reading they far surpassed the unselected children. However, the more highly gifted (IQ 170+) had experienced more problems of adjustment than had the more typically gifted. The divorce and death rates of the gifted group were below normal, and the marriage rate was normal. Health statistics were superior; 5% of the group admitted to having had mental health problems, but recovery rate was good. Politically, the group tended to be liberal-progressive.

This study laid the foundation for the modern understanding of giftedness. For this reason it is necessary to draw attention to a number of problems and special issues, although these do not detract from the pioneering contribution of Terman's work. There were problems with the sample he studied: Goleman (1980) pointed out that "Latin American, Italian and Portuguese groups were underrepresented, and there were only two Black children, two Armenians, and one American Indian child, (while) Jewish children were overrepresented." Further, "there was also a social class bias. Close to one out of three children were from professional families, although professionals made up only 3 percent of the general population. Only a smattering were children of unskilled laborers, compared with 15 percent in the general population" (p. 31). The group identified by Terman contained "a significant but not overwhelming preponderance of boys" (116 : 100 ratio of boys to girls at the elementary level, 160 : 100 at the high school level). It is also probable that emotionally maladjusted and underachieving students were overlooked.

Initially, Terman's teachers were asked to nominate the children in their classes whom they considered to be the brightest; the name of the youngest child in each class was also recorded. Terman later reported that "one of the most astonishing facts brought out of this investigation is that one's best chance of identifying the brightest child in a schoolroom is to examine the birth records and select the youngest rather than to take the one rated as brightest by the teacher" (see Jenkins & Paterson, 1961, p. 321). Nominated children from elementary schools were then screened by the use of group intelligence tests, and final selection was based on an individually administered Stanford-Binet test. Selection of high school gifted students was made on the basis of performance on the Terman Group Test, a derivative of the Stanford-Binet. Terman's own evaluation of the methods of "sifting" he employed was that "possibly 10 or 15 percent of the total number who could have qualified according to the criterion (a Stanford-Binet IQ of 140 or higher) were missed."

The "Freezing" of Thinking About Intelligence

Subsequently, the concept of intelligence gained widespread acceptance and exerted a great influence on education. The key point for the present purposes is that, despite all development of new tests and revision and updating that has occurred since, modern thinking about the nature of intelligence is based mainly on Binet's ideas. In fact, until recently the Stanford-Binet scale has provided the dominant operational definition of what is meant by the term *intelligence*. When a new test of intelligence was devised, the question of whether or not it really measured intelligence was settled by seeing whether scores on the new test closely resembled those of the same children on the Stanford-Binet scale. Thus, the criterion for whether a test measures intelligence has come to be whether the things it asks people to do resemble the tasks originally selected by Binet. Golann (1963) concluded that intelligence tests had not changed much for 60 or more years. Recent interest in creativity may well represent the first major and fundamental change in direction since the original formulations of Binet.

The influence of Binet's ideas has had a second and more subtle effect. Not only have the kinds of items he selected dominated thinking about the measurement of intelligence, but the kinds of mental functioning required to do well on Binet's scale have come to be regarded as synonymous with intelligence. He believed that an intelligent person is able to (a) take and maintain a definite direction in behavior (to act with purpose), (b) resist distractions (to concentrate), and (c) adopt new lines of attack when old ones fail (to correct mistakes). School children thus came to be regarded as more or less intelligent to the extent to which they were good at these kinds of mental functioning, and teachers came to esteem such functions (which would yield high scores on intelligence tests) above all others. Even more important, they strove to foster in their students the particular type of mental functioning needed to succeed on Binet like tasks. Thinking about the question of how human intellect functions was thus frozen into a particular mold.

A Classroom Example

The sort of thing which can happen when a student fails to conform to the model of strict reproduction of known "correct" material is exemplified in the following example.

The scene—In a high school geometry class the teacher is going over the previous day's quick test, which involved writing out from memory the proof of a theorem *that the angle subtended at the circumference by the diameter of a circle is a right angle*. The students were required to reproduce the textbook proof exactly. There were only two possible marks: 10 (for word perfect reproduction), and 0 for anything else. One student wrote out what looked like a valid proof, although quite different from that in the text, and received no marks. (Actually, his proof was incorrect, because it involved the use of another theorem, which is itself proved by assuming that the angle at the circumference is a right angle— that is, his proof contained a tautological error. However, this was not what the teacher was concerned about.) The student raises his hand and asks the teacher: "Couldn't you prove it by saying that…(he outlines his proof)?" Before he has gone very far, the teacher interrupts him. He remembers what the boy has written from grading it, and he knows that the mark of 0 was given. He wanted the students to reproduce the textbook solution exactly and did not even bother to check the details of the boy's work once he realized that it differed from the text. He shouts loudly: "Is that the way it is in the book, Smith?" Smith mumbles that it is not. "Well, then, why are you wasting our time reading out that nonsense?" Smith starts to explain that he thought it would work his way. The teacher begins to lose his temper. He asks coldly: "What do you think the person who marks your geometry exam would give you for that, young man? In case you don't know, I'll tell you. He'd give you exactly nothing, nothing at all!"

Smith now makes the mistake of sticking to his guns: "But I can't see what's wrong with doing it my way," he insists. "It comes out easily and doesn't take half as many lines." The teacher goes red. He is fed up with going over this boy's work with him, because he keeps on making this kind of interruption. He bellows: "I'm sick and tired of your nonsense. You think you know more than the book, do you? Well, Mr. Clever, I'll tell you what. If I have any more of your interruptions, you can go and tell the principal why you're too clever to accept the answer in the book. Now just shut up and let the rest of us who want to pass our exams get on with our work." Smith subsides. He has understood that passing the external examination is the first priority that the class faces. Getting ready for it is more important than following up his ideas. Above all, it is necessary to be right. He has also had a sharp lesson in the importance of keeping to the text and of accepting authority.

A BROADENED CONCEPT OF ABILITY

Convergent Thinking

Although many earlier writers published scattered and spasmodic state-ments in the area, it was not until Guilford's 1950 Presidential Address to the American Psychological Association that a systematic and influential questioning of the narrowness of thinking about the mental processes conventionally regarded as intelligent emerged. Guilford showed that a restricted conceptualization of intelligence was built into current intelligence testing, and hence into thinking about the nature of intellectual functioning. Subsequently, other writers such as Getzels and Jackson (1962) extended Guilford's arguments by showing that a similar narrowness of view permeates ideas, not only about intelligence tests, but about what kinds of processes constitute efficient and worthwhile thinking in school children. McLeod and Cropley (1989) offered a more detailed discussion, emphasizing the importance of broadening understanding of intellectual functioning in order to incorporate divergent thinking. Gardner (1983) and Sternberg (1985) have recently offered other broad models of intelligence.

In a nutshell, Guilford argued that conventional tests require almost exclusively the finding of a single best answer to a problem. This answer is always known in advance (for example, it is to be found in the test manual). The task of the person whose intelligence is being tested is really to arrive at answers which coincide with those in the scoring key. In fact, the major task is to use a variety of information provided in a test item to "close in" on one, and only one, "best" answer. For this reason, Guilford concluded that intelligence, as it has conventionally been conceptualized, actually involves what he called *convergent thinking*. The usual kind of task given to schoolchildren requires them to extract some formula or principle from a body of information and then to reapply that principle with the help of strictly conventional logic in order to yield a single correct answer. Usually tasks are highly speeded so that, to be deemed intelligent, it is necessary, not only to think convergently, but to work fast. In order to make certain that one and only one answer is possible, it is sometimes necessary to give very elaborate instructions concerning what may and may not be done. In at least one well-known conventional abilities test, reading through the restraints and conditions on some subsections of the test is assigned more time than doing the actual test itself!

Divergent Thinking

As Guilford pointed out, the outstanding feature of convergent thinking is that it involves recognition and reproduction of single best answers which are already known in advance. The thinker is not required to invent anything, to exercise ingenuity or originality, or to seek novel solutions. In fact, a child who does any of these things is likely to give different or unusual answers and therefore to be treated as unintelligent. Innovative thinking is operationally defined as unintelligent!

Fortunately, children and adults persistently introduce "incorrect," uncommon, or original lines of thought into solving problems. Most teachers have encountered children who come up with unexpected answers and can explain them with ingenious, compelling and clever supportive arguments. No matter how a situation is structured to try to make everybody think in the same way and to arrive at the same answers, children (and some adults too) persist in being contrary enough to follow individual lines of thought that lead to idiosyncratic ideas! For the designers of convergent thinking tests, this trait is an annoyance that has not yet been successfully stamped out. However, as Guilford argued, it may well be as worthy of respect and high esteem as convergent thinking. He then pressed the claims of what he called *divergent thinking*, suggesting that this latter kind of thinking should be given serious consideration. The main feature of divergent thinking is that people "branch out" from known information to generate many new ideas of their own. Divergent-thinking tests impose minimal constraints that structure and shape ideas. The task of the people being taught is to produce large numbers of ideas which they have invented for themselves. Right and wrong are never known in advance, and instead of emphasis being on single, best, correct answers, it is on production of many different ideas. Two children may give totally different answers to a divergent thinking test but be judged to have performed equally well. A child may generate one of more answers which the person scoring the test has never seen before; far from being dismissed as incorrect, the answer may be highly valued. Divergent thinking branches out from the known and produces novel ideas.

The essence of convergent thinking, by contrast, is the "zeroing in" on the one—and only one—"best" answer. This answer can be reached by applying known logic in a systematic fashion to a set of clues. With

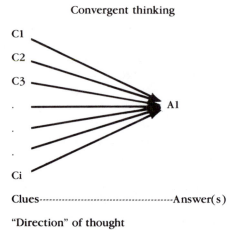

Convergent thinking

C1

C2

C3

.

.

.

Ci

A1

Clues---Answer(s)

"Direction" of thought

sufficient knowledge of the facts, and the ability to discern the underlying rules, the one best answer can be determined. Many appropriately informed people taking the same item would all reach the same answer. The convergent-thinking process can thus be conceptualized as having the form shown.

In order to bring out how different it is from convergent thinking, a schematic representation of divergent thinking is shown below.

Divergent Thinking

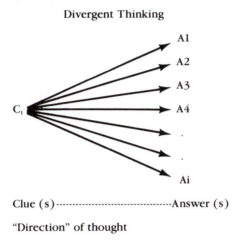

Clue (s) ----------------------------------Answer (s)

"Direction" of thought

CASE STUDIES

Guilford's approach launched a wave of interest and offered an initial way of looking at the psychology of creativity. The two case studies presented below show the dramatic differences (not only in the cognitive domain) between "divergers" and "convergers." They are based on studies presented in Cropley (1967a).

Tom was a school boy aged 11 years 1 month. He was about to enter the eighth grade and had achieved this advanced status at the age of 11 by "skipping" grades along the way: he was, in fact, a full 2 years younger than the average age of his classmates. He was a smallish, slightly overweight boy and totally uninterested in sport. However, his smallness was exaggerated by his comparative youth—physically he was a sound specimen. Both his parents were graduates and had lived apart for several years, Tom being raised from an early age by his mother alone. She was an energetic woman who dominated the boy at all times: she told him when he might play, when he must do homework, when he must read "good" novels, and so on. She insisted that he must play chess with her at a given time each evening, insisted on a certain schedule for piano practice (Tom played mechanically—technically well, but lifelessly), and ran his life completely. She administered severe corporal punishment for trivial offenses and was domineering, controlling, intrusive, and authoritarian.

Tom liked listening to classical music but detested "modern" music. His favorite school subject was hard to choose, as he liked them all, but it was probably mathematics. His hobby was chess. Although he did not like sport and was no good at it, he was prepared to do his best. He was shy and timid, causing his playmates a great deal of embarrassment by the rapidity with which he was reduced to tears. Otherwise he kept his feelings very much to himself and had virtually no really close friends. This state of affairs continued throughout his school and university days. He was extremely amibitious and very hard-working. He took his schoolwork very seriously and would sulk for days, or even cry, if he did badly in a test. His level of expectation of himself was so high that he regarded less than 100% as a failure.

Although they tended to describe him as a "bit of a baby" and mostly admitted that they could not really get to like him as a person, Tom's teachers spoke enthusiastically when asked about him. He was invariably described as a "pleasure to teach," "a willing and able boy," "an ornament to the classroom," and so on. He was obedient and well-behaved and was, you might say, the apple of the teachers' eyes. His best subjects were math, science, and Latin. He produced grammatically perfect, stylistically dull work for his English teacher, who found him word perfect but uninspired.

Tom was a brilliant student. As his high school career progressed, he went from success to success. He topped his entire state in every major exam for which he sat and invariably carried off first place in most individual subjects, although he was never the top in English. He did not take any subjects like art but concentrated on more "academic" courses. He completed high school too young for admission to university and was obliged to spend an extra year at school, during which he took up several entirely new subjects at the grade-12 level and handled them with ease in 1 year instead of 6 or 7. He easily won a university place on the basis of his second high school graduation grades, although he had only taken up the subjects 1 year previously. His career through university was similarly brilliant, and he gained first or second place every year in every subject. At present, he is a professional man in a large city, and is doing well. It is interesting to notice that he is merely at the middle of his profession and has failed to make the same kind of mark he did when he was a student. He has made no contribution, either theoretical or empirical, to his profession.

Kath was an attractive, rather sophisticated girl, aged 16 years 1 month. She had an older brother and an older sister who both attended college. Her parents had both had some university training. Kathy's interests included art, sculpture, and music. She was also a keen sportswoman and was very interested in social contacts with boys. She liked classical music, folk music, and jazz, and her main hobbies were playing the guitar (folk music), playing the piano, and collecting art prints. Her favorite school subject was art, and her ambition was to become an art teacher.

Kathy's IQ was 119, derived from a verbal score of 113 and a performance score of 121. Specific abilities, expressed in such a form that average ability earns a 5 (SD = 1), included nonverbal ability 5.9, speed and accuracy 6.2, and perceptual and spatial ability 6.5. On the Torrance Tests of Creative Thinking she obtained the highest scores for originality of a group of 200 high school students with whom she was tested. She scored 57 for Originality of Figures, compared with an average score of 29.4 for the whole group, and 88 for Originality of Titles, almost four times the average score of 22.2. Although these scores indicated that Kathy was of high average IQ and had a number of well-developed specific abilities, her scores on conventional tests were by no means commensurate with her creativity scores. These latter suggested that she was perhaps one in a thousand as far as creativity is concerned, but her IQ scores placed her as merely one in six or thereabouts.

The Rorschach test was administered to Kathy, and the data interpreted "blindly" by an independent rater who had no personal knowledge of who Kathy was or of why she was being tested. The interpretation of the Rorschach data indicated that she was essentially a theoretical type, but that she retained reasonable contact with the practical requirements of a situation. She revealed a sensitive self-awareness and a need for warm personal relationships, accompanied by a tendency for free emotional expression and uncontrolled emotion. Nevertheless, she was essentially an extroverted person, despite her interest in her own emotions and her willingness to express them freely. Finally, responses to the test indicated that she was ambitions and could push herself hard in her schoolwork in seeking success.

Kathy's various teachers were asked to report on her as a pupil and also as a person. Her teachers in mathematics and science reported that she was normal in her classroom behavior and that she was not excessively noisy or inattentive. Her science teacher commented on her tendency to get very enthusiastic about portions of the course and to put an unusual amount of work into anything which caught her imagination (for example, a project in geology). This teacher also commented on Kathy's high levels of initiative and drive. The French teacher found Kathy friendly and respectful, and commented favorably on her positive personality. This point was also emphasized by the teacher who took her for English and history. This teacher mentioned that Kathy "has definite opinions on things" and that she possessed "a strong personality." Although opportunities for creative work were limited at the level at which Kathy was studying, her English teacher was particularly struck by the high quality of her creative production and commented too on her eagerness to "delve into things." All teachers were satisfied with Kathy's school work and rated it "good" or "satisfactory." It was the comments of Kathy's art teacher, however, which were really enthusiastic. This teacher described her as outstanding. She was "a rewarding child to teach" and was "creative, with an all-round talent in art." These comments echoed the report of Kathy's capacities which had accompanied her on her move to high school from her elementary school. On this report, she was described as "artistic, reliable, versatile."

These case studies describe two youngsters of markedly different "styles." Such differences are by no means isolated instances: Hudson (1966) reported a large number of examples of pairs of boys who could be contrasted in the same way, some preferring the convergent style, some the divergent. Several clear-cut differences emerge from the data on Tom and Kathy, the most obvious being in the intellectual domain. However, differences between the two were by no means confined to this aspect but were accompanied by differences on a number of other variables, some of which may even play a causal role in the intellectual differences.

The difference in the capacity of the two young people to handle their own emotions is very clear-cut. Tom never showed emotion, except when it was out of control. At other times he kept it bottled up. On the other hand, Kathy expressed emotion freely and yet in a controlled way. In their relationships with other people, they were also more or less opposites. Tom was socially inept; Kathy was very skilled. Such differences may well reflect the different childrearing practices of the two sets of parents. An inventory administered to Kathy's parents indicated that they believed strongly in fostering egalitarianism and comradeship, and that they approved of her activities. They were strongly opposed to fostering dependency, breaking the will, and intrusiveness. Tom's mother was punitive and domineering and completely destroyed her son's independence and spirit. She drove him to achieve outstanding performance in academic pursuits and regulated all his spare time. On the other hand, Kathy's parents were permissive and fostered independence in their daughter. Although these two students are extreme examples, there is a good deal of evidence to suggest that there is a systematic relationship between parental practices in rearing their children and the degree of creativity manifested by those children.

FURTHER READING

Eysench, H.J. (1979). *The structure and measurement of intelligence.* Berlin: Springer.

Feldman, D.H. (1980). *Beyond universals in cognitive development.* Norwood, NJ: Ablex.

Gardner, H. (1983). *Frames of mind: The theory of multiple intelligences.* New York: Basic Books.

Sternberg, R.J., & Detterman, D.K. (Eds.). (1986). *What is intelligence?* Norwood, NJ: Ablex.

Wallach, M.A. (1971). *The intelligence/creativity distinction.* New York: General Learning Press.

4

Defining and Measuring Creativity

Defining *creativity* is difficult—as difficult as defining intelligence. The term is applied to people, processes, and products (Barron & Harrington, 1981). Wallach (1985) concluded that a narrow definition (for instance, performance in a particular area) yields the most convincing findings, because results become less and less clear-cut as the definition becomes more general. By contrast, Simonton (1988) argued in favor of a general theory of creativity, as did the Soviet researcher Altshuller (1984). Of course, a general theory cannot encompass all details of specific creative performances. For instance, although the theory might specify that "task-relevant skills" are necessary for creative solutions, a painter would need different skills from those required by, let us say, a mathematician. Campbell (1960) and, more recently, Weisberg (1986) and Simonton (1988), have gone so far as to argue that most elements of the conventional creativity concept (for instance, divergent thinking) are unnecessary. Despite all this, the term is used in everyday language without excessive difficulty or confusion, while the role of creativity in high achievement, as well as ways of fostering and training it in the classroom, have become major topics in modern educational discussions.

McLeod and Cropley (1989) identified five general elements which are necessary for creativity, even if they do not offer an exhaustive definition; *novelty* or originality, *relevance, effectiveness, ethical desirability,* and *communication.* The first element is decisive in distinguishing creativity from, for instance, facility, speed, accuracy, wealth of information, and so on, these latter being characteristic of "mere" intelligence. Although they may well facilitate the emergence of creativity, or even be necessary for it to occur, it is novelty which is decisive. At the same time, this novelty is not simply wild, outrageous, or random: It must help in coping with some special situation, even if its relevance and effectiveness are not at first obvious—creativity may sometimes only be recognized years (or even centuries) later. In practical terms, some form of communication is necessary; otherwise, creativity would remain hidden. Finally, the positive social value associated with the term *creativity,* along with the presence of an ethical element in education, make it repugnant to speak of the creativity of a cheat, a mass murderer, or an evil demagogue.

The Criterion Problem

It has repeatedly been shown that the concept of intelligence has effectively delimited, not only the most successful students and the best achievers in the academic world, but also those people most effective in human relationship and in a wide variety of other socially approved activities. Humphreys (1985) emphasized that intelligence is still central to the whole idea of gifts and talents, and Stanley (1984) concluded that an IQ score is still the best single indicator of intellectual potential. Nonetheless, the conventional concept has been criticized, as has already been shown, because it refers only to a narrow band of intellectual abilities. An early statement to this effect was that of Getzels and Jackson (1962). Since then many other authors have made a similar point (e.g., Gardner, 1983). The success of IQs in predicting school success may well be the result of the concept of intelligence having had the criterion built into it (Cattell, 1963). In the light of these and other criticisms, *creativity* has recently gained wide acceptance as an alternative to *intelligence.*

However, a problem immediately arises: establishing a criterion of creativity. Just what is regarded as creative varies not only from society to society, but from age to age. Thus, in Victorian England it was deemed necessary to expurgate Shakespeare's works. Similarly, the extraordinary creativity of the French mathematician Galois was not recognized until many years after his death. A large number of similar examples exist. In the face of this problem, attempts to study creativity have utilized such criteria as production of works generally acknowledged as creative, such as a poem or a novel, public acclaim for creative eminence, active pursuit of pastimes generally acknowledged to be creative, and so on. Studies of persons selected because they had produced works of a kind generally acknowledged to be creative include those of Cropley and Sikand (1973), Drevdahl and Cattell (1958), Eiduson (1958), Freud (1910), MacKinnon (1983), and Simonton (1988).

However, it seems likely that creativity may manifest itself in a variety of styles. For teachers, one important form of creativity is not that of producing creative solutions oneself, but of energizing and crystallizing creative effort in others. Creativity also ranges across a wide variety of fields, so that it is necessary to take account of creativity in science, mathematics, engineering, and so on, as well as artistic creativity. Presumably the development of the Land Polaroid camera, or Poincaré's mathematical equations, represents creativity just as much as the act of painting the Mona Lisa. Barron (1969) reviewed the various forms that creativity may take, including the ability to crystallize it in other people. Wallach (1985) concluded that creativity can only be studied by concentrating on a specific field, but Altshuller (1984) argued for a general theory of creativity. McLeod and Cropley (1989) offer a review of this area.

Apart from the problem of areas of creativity, further difficulties arise out of questions such as, "For whom should some product or idea be novel? For the apparently creative person himself or herself, for a narrow circle of expert observers, for all of society, or … ?" One way of dealing with this issue has been to speak of *levels of creativity* (Taylor, 1975). At the lowest level is "expressive spontaneity," which is to be found in, for instance, the uninhibited production of ideas often seen in young children. Originality and quality of the product are unimportant at this level. Higher levels include "technical" creativity, which is characterized by unusual skill or proficiency; "inventive" creativity, in which the already known is utilized in novel ways; "innovative" creativity, which requires that existing principles be taken a step further; and, finally, "emergent" creativity, in which completely new abstract principles are recognized and stated.

In an approach which concentrates more on psychological properties of the people involved, Sternberg (1988) distinguished six *facets* of creativity: "insight" (leading to effective selection of information), "knowledge" (which provides a stock of information out of which selection is possible), "personal factors" (e.g., flexibility, tenacity, willingness to take risks), "courage of one's convictions," "intrinsic motivation," and "relevance." According to these analyses, not only a recognized world expert but also a young child who showed knowledge of the appropriate material, insight, flexibility, "stickability," and determination in producing a relevant idea could be said to be "creative," even if at vastly different levels (cf. Cohen, 1989).

The need for relevance emphasizes that creative thinking should lead to worthwhile results. This property distinguishes it from blind unconventionality or simple expressive spontaneity. Among others, Bruner (1962), Motamedi (1982), and Sappington and Farrar (1982) emphasized the necessity for creative products to have a close relationship to reality. Creativity should lead to "effective surprise" (Bruner, 1962). However, it is important to keep ethical and moral issues in mind (McLaren, in press). Is it creative, for example, for a burglar to apply the principles of electronic engineering in an unprecedented way to develop a device for nullifying burglar alarms? Is the burglar as creative as an engineer who, showing a similar degree of novelty, effectiveness, and the like, develops a foolproof burglar alarm?

Creativity as a "Style"

The term *creativity* is currently used in two senses. The first is the person-in-the-street usage, in which creativity involves end products hailed by knowledgeable people as creative (a painting, piece of music, or a novel). The word *creativity* in its general usage thus strongly implies the existence of end products that meet some social, professional, or aesthetic criterion. However, the term is also used by teachers to refer to a capacity to be inventive, original, and innovative (i.e., to think divergently). Children are said to be creative if they have many and varied ideas, if they see relationships that are not usually noticed, or if they devise unusual solutions to problems. This usage is adhered to by teachers and parents to refer to creativity both with and without high levels of artistic, literary, musical, or scientific/technical output (i.e., with and without tangible, socially recognized end products). In this book, teachers will be regarded as fostering creativity in children when they encourage their capacity and willingness to think divergently, without necessarily requiring that the children start producing prize winning literary works, paintings to be hung in the Museum of Modern Art, or similar products of the creative process.

About 20 years ago I began arguing for a conceptualization of creativity as a *way of applying* intellectual ability, not as an ability in its own right—creativity as a "style" of thinking. Other writers have described it as a "form of application" of intelligence (Gardner, 1983) or a "way of re-organizing" ideas (Horowitz & O'Brien, 1986). To oversimplify, people can prefer to attack mental tasks in a convergent (reapplying the already known and seeking the best solution) or a divergent (branching out and trying the new) way. All pupils are in principle capable of both styles, regardless of their IQ, although their experiences may have inculcated a strong preference for the one or other style (usually the convergent). A one-sided preference for convergence (or, for that matter, for divergence) thus represents a narrowing of intellectual activity rather than a quantitative decrease.

The teacher who wishes to foster creativity in students can therefore begin by developing in them a more rounded pattern of intelligence, by promoting divergent as well as convergent thinking. This task may consist of removing obstacles to divergent thinking, as well as providing positive incentives for it (Runco, 1990, chap. 20). The practical suggestions in this book often contain advice concerning the encouragement of divergent thinking and are not necessarily linked to developing creativity in the aesthetic/professional sense. Of course, adoption of this relatively modest aim does not mean that the procedures may not help to promote creativity in the broader sense. Many teachers may wish to set their sights on the more difficult target. However, the thrust of the present book is primarily towards fostering a wider range of psychological processes in the classroom. This is because fostering creativity in the divergent-thinking sense is beginning to be relatively well understood, and more emphasis on it is needed in view of the one-sided conceptualization of intelligence to date. This goal is also one which lies reasonably within the powers of schoolteachers and parents.

The Quantitative Approach

A further problem that has bedevilled research studies in the area of creativity has been that of whether creativity is something that is present in all people, albeit to a greater or lesser extent in some than in others, or whether it is something that people either have or do not have. Basically, two opposed points of view can be seen. The first of these holds that creative people differ from other people in a *qualitative* sense—they are a different kind of person, following a different path of mental, social, and personal functioning. The creative processes are then seen as mystical, spiritual, unknowable, untestable, and incapable of being studied or written about in any systematic or useful manner. Indeed, books such as the present one amount almost to sacrilege when viewed from the point of view of this "spiritual" model.

Contrasting with the spiritual model is the view that creative people differ from noncreatives merely in a *quantitative* way—that is, the processes and personal properties underlying the creative style are simple extensions of states and processes present, to some extent at least, in all people. Perkins (1981) concluded that when people *not* recognized as creative attempt to solve problems, they go through the same stages of thinking as do poets, artists, and inventors. The difference is one of degree and purpose, not of kind. In a nutshell, it is argued that everybody is capable of functioning in a creative way—of thinking divergently, seeking the novel, innovative and original, and enjoying branching out from the old and well known. Thus, the quantitative model of creativity implies that "creativity" is present, at least as a potential, in all people, if only they can be encouraged to manifest it.

Adoption of either a qualitative or a quantitative model of creativity is much more important than merely the settling of an academic argument. The two views have vastly different implications for "remedial" measures. The qualitative model implies that creative people possess something that others do not, and that, if any special attempt is to be made to develop creativity, it should concentrate on the members of the chosen group. (Indeed, simply leaving the creative alone to do their stuff in peace might be the best tactic!) By contrast, the quantitative model assumes that all people are capable of adopting a creative style, and thus implies that society should try to bring out the latent creativity in all of its citizens, if creativity really is important.

This latter position is clearly more productive from the point of view of everyday classroom teachers going about their normal business. It suggests that the teacher has a role to play with all students in the area of creativity. This role involves defining the psychological bases of creativity, identifying the aspects of classroom organization that act upon these bases, and trying to modify that organization in such a way as to foster whatever potentials for creativity exist in all students. It is precisely this attitude to creativity (the quantitative model), and this purpose (identification and modification of classroom behaviors with the aim of increasing creative functioning in all students), that underly the present volume.

CREATIVITY TESTS

Associated with increasing interest among teachers in creativity has been an increasing interest in development of creativity tests. If testing has been one-sided, why not redress the balance by developing creativity tests? Such tests would also have the advantage of providing a concrete, operational definition of creativity, in much the same way as intelligence tests reified the concept of intelligence. A substantial number of creativity tests already existed before the commencement of the modern era (see McLeod & Cropley, 1989, for a review), but these will not be discussed here. Initial developments in recent times concentrated on measuring divergent thinking: Subjects are confronted with an apparently simple situation and asked to generate a large number of ideas arising from the situation (for instance: "List as many uses as you can for a tin can"). Emphasis in scoring is on *number* (measured by counting the number of suggestions) and *quality* (in the sense of degree of "divergence," usually measured by giving high scores to answers which are statistically uncommon). Guilford (1967) himself designed procedures such as the "Alternative Uses Test," the "Product Improvement Test," and the "Consequences Test." These and similar tests were extended and refined in what are now known as the Torrance Tests of Creative Thinking (Torrance, 1974). Wallach and Kogan (1965) altered both the administration procedure for such tests and the method of scoring, while essentially retaining the basic model: Their tests were administered in a gamelike setting without time limits, and scoring emphasized answers which were unique within a given group of subjects. Another early test which took a somewhat different line of approach, while continuing to emphasize unusual associations, was Mednick's (1962) Remote Associates Test.

Similar tests appeared in Europe, including the Test zum divergenten Denken (Meinberger, 1977) and the Verbaler Kreativitätstest (Schoppe, 1975) in German, and the Espressioni test (Calvi, 1966) in Italy. It has repeatedly been pointed out that such tests have only a low level of face validity (they do not resemble what common sense suggests creativity is like), because they seem to have little in common with the kind of mental activities involved in painting the Mona Lisa or writing, say, *Gone With the Wind* (see Schubert, Wagner, & Schubert, 1988, for a recent discussion). Zarnegar, Hocevar, and Michael (1988) recently suggested a number of revisions of the classical tests mentioned above, and provided an extensive review of the validity of scores (also see Runco, 1991). However, attempts to develop creativity tests that really do measure creativity have been plagued by the criterion problems already mentioned. This has led to several approaches to demonstrating their validity.

Relationship with Conventional Tests

One major attempt to deal with this problem has been to compare scores on creativity tests with those on intelligence tests, and to show that creativity tests sort people out in a somewhat different way from intelligence -tests. A summary of the relationship of creativity tests and conventional tests can be found in McLeod and Cropley (1989). In general there are significant correlations, as high as about 0.75. Wallach (1970) showed that correlations between IQs and "creativity" scores are high when the "creativity" test measures verbal fluency, but markedly lower when fluency in getting ideas is emphasized. Nonetheless, it has been shown that selection of talented individuals purely on the basis of IQ overlooks a substantial group of people who obtain high scores on creativity tests but not on intelligence tests. Torrance (1962) pointed out that equating high ability purely with high IQ would overlook about 20% of the most highly creative people, a finding Hitchfield (1973) confirmed in a study conducted in Great Britain. I myself identified groups of highly creative people with relatively low IQ scores among both schoolchildren in Canada and university students in Australia (Cropley, 1967a, b).

Early statistical studies of the relationship between scores on intelligence tests (usually IQs) and those on creativity tests indicated that they are often substantial, although some creativity tests seem to be closely interrelated with each other but relatively independent of IQ. For instance, Wallach and Kogan (1965) reported greater independence from intelligence for their tests. When groups of individuals preselected for high intelligence are studied, virtually zero interrelationships between creativity scores and IQs are obtained (Yamamoto, 1965). Although there are certain technical problems with this finding, it has supported the notion that there is a threshold of IQ beyond which creativity and intelligence become completely independent of each other. The threshold approach is usually attributed to MacKinnon (1965) and was more recently reviewed by Runco and Albert (1986). This purported threshold has been set as low as 120 and as high as 140.

Creativity Tests and Academic Achievement

A second attempt to validate creativity tests has involved examining relationships between test scores and achievement in school. An early and heuristically important study in this field was that of Getzels and Jackson (1962). They showed that academic achievement among high school students selected because they obtained very high scores on creativity tests, but not on intelligence tests, was as good as that of students selected because they obtained high scores on intelligence tests, but not creativity tests. However, this study has been subjected to a great deal of criticism, mainly on methodological grounds. Nonetheless, other writers have reported similar findings: Both Wallach and Kogan (1965) and Cropley (1972) showed that creativity test scores did add to the prediction of school achievement. Maslany (1973) showed that this relationship between creativity test scores and achievement is not confined to more creative aspects of school curriculum, but that it is no stronger than the contribution of IQ scores.

A mass of studies, mostly in North America, beginning in the 1950s showed low correlations between school achievement and creativity test scores (see Torrance, 1962, 1963, for examples). In the United Kingdom, Haddon and Lytton (1968) reported similar findings, and in the Federal Republic of Germany and Switzerland Krause (1972, 1977) showed that correlations between creativity scores and grades were as low as .09 (Phys. Ed.) or .15 (Art). In a longitudinal study from the 7th to the 11th grade in West Germany, Sierwald (1989) reported similar findings: Not only was the correlation between creativity test scores and school marks actually negative in the case of Physics (− 0.12), but it did not rise above 0.26, even for Art.

A problem in such studies is that academic achievement may be an inappropriate criterion against which to validate creativity tests, because it is itself essentially noncreative. Some researchers have attempted to meet this problem by utilizing a more "creative" criterion of academic achievement. One study (Cropley, 1967b) examined the admission of male science specialists to honors programs in an Australian university. It showed that, although high scorers on creativity tests were not distinguished from low scorers in their achievement in early university years, they provided a disproportionately high number of the students who were admitted to honors programs. Furthermore, the persons responsible for making the selections claimed that they looked for "creativity" as one of the main criteria. Thus, there is a suggestion that creativity tests are superior predictors of academic achievement when the criterion of creativity is expressly taken into account.

Creativity Tests and Achievement in Life

This line of though has been reinforced by studies of people acknowledged to have displayed creativity in their real adult lives. One common method of identifying such people has been to ask members of a particular profession, such as architects or research scientists, to make up lists of the most creative workers in their field. The most frequently identified people are then contacted and asked to participate in the research. For example, Helson and Crutchfield (1970) asked practising mathematicians to nominate people who had made significant creative contributions to their discipline. The highly creative mathematicians were then compared with mathematicians of ordinary creativity, such factors as age and status of the institutions at which they had received their training being carefully matched. It was found that there were no significant differences in the IQ scores obtained by the highly creative and the less creative scholars.

Other reports have supplemented these findings by showing that many people who have been recognized as highly creative in adult life have not been exceptional in terms of grades at school. A study by MacKinnon (1983) examined the early lives of people who later became creative, and showed that they did not obtain significantly higher marks in high school than other students. McLeod and Cropley (1989) mentioned a number of studies of eminent creative people who had difficulty in school: Examples include Einstein, Schubert, Shaw, Tolstoy, Delius, Gandhi, and Nehru. Two famous examples of this phenomenon are Albert Einstein, who was notably poor at mathematics at school, and Winston Churchill, who received poor reports from his English teachers! Even grades at university do not necessarily distinguish between those who eventually become highly creative and those who do not (e.g., Cropley, 1967b). It has been suggested that the absence of a relationship between real-life creativity and academic grades results from the fact that school and university curricula concentrate on fostering and rewarding convergent thinking.

Where the criterion is more clearly related to creativity, results suggest that creativity tests are more useful. Vaughan (1971) reported that students with higher creativity scores did better on a measure of musical creativity, and Sadek (1986) obtained a correlation between musical talent and creativity tests scores of 0.20. However, in both cases the music score involved a music test, not published music or some similar real-life criterion. To demonstrate convincingly that so-called "creativity" tests really do measure creativity, a long-term predictive study of the kind conducted by Terman in connection with intelligence tests is necessary (e.g., Terman, 1925). What is needed is to examine the behavior of people previously identified as high scorers on creativity tests, and to show that they are creative in their real lives. Evidence that such persons subsequently followed pursuits of a creative kind, or succeeded in achievements acknowledged as creative, would be very compelling.

One study along these lines related scores on creativity tests administered on admission to university to what were called "nonacademic talented accomplishments" during the high school years which had just been completed (Wallach & Wing, 1969). The criterion data on out-of-school achievements were derived from a questionnaire asking for information about activities in such areas as leadership, art, music, and so on. An incidental finding was that, as it consistently reported in the literature, school achievement and IQ were closely related. The study showed that nonacademic accomplishments were not significantly related to IQ. However, the major finding was that students classified as high scorers on the creativity tests obtained significantly higher scores for out-of-school achievements in the creative areas studied. Encouraging but inconclusive results have also been reported in more recent studies. Sierwald (1989), for instance, reported a correlation of 0.20 between out-of-school accomplishments and creativity test scores in a group of German high school students. Okuda, Runco, and Berger (1990) reported coefficients of approximately .50 using divergent thinking tasks containing "real-world" problems.

A longitudinal study in Canada (Cropley, 1972) involved administration of a battery of creativity tests to 350 grade 7 students. It should be mentioned at this point, however, that the creativity tests were scored only on the dimension of originality, which some writers have concluded contains the "essence of creativity." Subsequently, two follow-up studies were carried out with this group, one after the passage of 5 years, the other after 7. In the 5-year follow-up, the subgroup studied at this time completed a questionnaire giving information about their nonacademic talented accomplishments during the year immediately preceding retesting (i.e., the fifth year since the original administration of the creativity tests). Nonacademic talent was assessed in the four areas of art, drama, literature, and music, areas of artistic rather than scientific or technological creativity. Findings indicated that the creativity tests had predicted later creative behavior, although the relationship was not clear-cut, and the conclusions have been criticized. Subsequently, the 5-year findings have been seriously questioned in a 7-year study (Maslany, 1973), in which the earlier project was extended by relocating 151 of the original group and obtaining from them information concerning their nonacademic accomplishments since grade 7. This study suggested that neither conventional IQs nor creativity test scores significantly predicted creative achievement, except for a correlation between IQ and music (cf. Hocevar, 1981; Runco, in press).

One of the most famous researchers in the area of creativity, Torrance, conducted several longitudinal studies covering periods of 6, 7, and even 22 years (e.g., Torrance, 1980). Although acknowledging weaknesses, he concluded that creativity tests really had measured aspects of human ability not satisfactorily covered by conventional tests. A study replicating aspects of Torrance's work in Australia (Howieson, 1981) came to the conclusion that creativity tests predicted life achievements 10 years later for boys, but not for girls; this is similar to one of the findings in the Canadian study described above. Nonetheless, studies which have compared the ability of creativity tests to predict later creative accomplishments with that of conventional intelligence tests have reported that creativity scores are useful, but no more useful than IQs. A possible resolution of conflicting conclusions is to be found in the fact that the more a test concentrates on a specific area of creativity (e.g., music or creative writing), and the more the criterion comes from the same area, the better the prediction. More general "creativity" scores, however, are no more valuable than IQs.

Creativity and Forming Ideas

What do creativity tests measure, then? This question has been extensively reviewed by Wallach (1970). He showed that two apparently contradictory sets of findings are consistently reported in the literature. At one extreme are reports of high internal consistency among creativity tests and low relationships with intelligence tests; at the other are findings reporting significant relationships among creativity tests and intelligence tests. By the time of the review in question, a sufficient number of studies of the two kinds was in existence to permit determining what was common to studies within each of the two groups. Wallach concluded that independence from conventional intelligence tests is obtained when the creativity tests emphasize getting large numbers of ideas, whereas high correlations with intelligence tests result when emphasis is on size of vocabulary or even skill in using words. He then suggested that this conclusion reemphasizes the need for creativity tests to be administered without time limits, as such limits necessarily limit ideational fluency (and hence creativity) by cutting off the flow of ideas. Thus, emphasis has now returned to the ability to get many ideas as a key element in creative thinking, a point made by Guilford (1967) in his original description of the mental abilities involved in divergent thinking. Guilford (1967) listed eight abilities, of which four ("Word Fluency," "Associational Fluency," "Ideational Fluency," and "Expressive Fluency") were abilities involving getting ideas.

Newer Tests

More recent tests have attempted to measure creativity in terms of specific models of internal psychological processes. Urban and Jellen (1986) designed the Test for Creative Thinking—Drawing Production, which differs from the tests described above in that scores are derived, not from the statistical uncommonness of verbal or figural associations, but from what the authors call "image production." Although respondents are asked to complete incomplete figures, as in several other tests, scoring is based, not on the unusualness of the figures created, but on nine psychological aspects of creativity derived from Gestalt psychology. These include "boundary breaking," "proportion of new elements," and "humor." Adopting a psychoanalytic approach, the Swedish psychologist Smith (see Smith & Carlsson, 1989) developed the Creative Functioning Test. This test regards creativity as dependent upon the ability to communicate with one's own subjective world, and involves gradually prolonged tachistoscopic exposure of a still life painting. Rothenberg's (1983) test of *Janusian thinking* is based on the idea that creative people are particularly good at bringing apparently incompatible ideas into a state of harmony via *homospatial thinking*. In one version of his test, stimulus words are exposed to subjects for very short periods; the subjects' are required to make verbal associations to these words, and scoring is based on the number of associations opposite in meaning to the original stimulus word to which they were offered.

An important advance in creativity testing in recent years derives from increasing recognition of the fact that creative production depends, not only on divergent thinking, but also on convergent thinking. This point of view has already been emphasized in several places in earlier sections. Facaoaru (1985) called for a "two track" testing procedure, which assesses the "area of overlap" between the two kinds of thinking. The Divergent-Convergent Problem Solving Processes Scale (Facaoaru & Bittner, 1987) assesses, among others, "goal-directed divergent thinking," "flexibility," and "task commitment." Very recently, Sternberg (1991) made a similar point (although he was concerned with the more general issue of intellectual abilities and did not focus on creativity) in discussing the Triarchic Ability Test. In general, the view that an adequate assessment of intellectual ability requires measurement of creativity as an intellectual component of giftedness seems to be finding increasing acceptance. In European discussions of psychological diagnosis, this view has been put with particular vigor by König (1986).

Personal Characteristics

Another approach that differs from the conventional emphasis on cognitive skills is to look at the degree of presence or absence of special personal characteristics that are thought to be necessary for creative thinking: independence, impulsiveness, self-confidence, and the like, or willingness to expend unusual levels of effort in pursuing interests. Ratings on such traits may be carried out by teachers or parents, even by peers, or they may take the form of self-ratings (Renzulli, Reis, & Smith, 1981; Rimm & Davis, 1980; Runco, 1989). The Scale for Rating Behavioral Characteristics of Superior Students (Renzulli, Reis, & Smith, 1981) is filled out by peers, and the Things My Child Likes to Do (Renzulli, Reis, & Smith, 1981) and the Parental Evaluation of Children's Creativity (Runco, 1989) are scales for parents. An example of a self-rating scale is the Gifted Inventory for Finding Talent (Rimm & Davis, 1980). A fuller review of instruments focusing on personal characteristics is to be found in Barron and Harrington (1981).

Another approach is to look at children's interests. Renzulli's (1977) Interest-Analyzer includes self-reports on participation in 35 creative activities. Another instrument emphasizing interests is McGreevy's (1982) Interest Questionnaire. A closely related approach involves the use of biographical inventories, of which Taylor and Ellison's (1978) Alpha Biographical Inventory is an example. Instruments of the kind just outlined can be seen as emphasizing the antecedents of creative behavior and in this sense are potentially of great value, not simply in identifying creative individuals, but in helping to specify the conditions which foster the growth of creativity. On the other hand, Hocevar's (1980) critical evaluation of the practical usefulness of instruments for measuring creativity led to the conclusion that actual creative achievements are the best criterion.

CASE STUDIES

The example which follows is based on a real incident. It illustrates the way in which teachers are often disconcerted by unexpected, divergent behavior and shows how their reactions may block the development of such thinking by discouraging, punishing, or ridiculing it. In contrast to the negative or blocking nature of the teacher's reaction (which actually occurred), an alternative, positive approach has been suggested. The setting is a third grade classroom. The children have been told by their teacher to make drawings of "a person's head." (Actually, she wants them to keep quiet for a quarter of an hour while she gets some paperwork done, but that has nothing to do with the story.) After several minutes one child comes out to her table with his drawing and asks for help, as he cannot remember what part to draw in a certain position. The teacher looks impatiently at his drawing, and is horrified to see that he has drawn *the inside* of a head. (He got the idea from TV commercials advertising a cough remedy.)

Blocking response. The teacher becomes angry and quickly concentrates the attention of the whole class on him while she castigates him for his stupidity. "What on earth is wrong with you, you silly little boy? How many times do I have to tell you before you get things right? You are always the nuisance who can't get things right. You couldn't draw a proper head like everybody else, could you? All the other children knew what I meant, but not you. Why didn't you draw a head the same as everyone else's?"

The boy is crushed and cowed, as he thought that it would be a good idea to draw the inside. He expected the teacher to praise him, and half of his reason for asking for help was that he wanted to make sure she saw what he had done. She regarded his unusual effort as a nuisance and a sign of naughtiness, especially as he often showed distinct signs of nonconformity in his thinking. In the past she had gradually developed a determination to make him fit in and do things the right way, the same as all the "good" children did. On this occasion he learned the first of many painful lessons about divergent work. He may soon learn to fear being different, hide anything unusual about himself and his work, and seek anonymity in a blanket of sameness.

Opening response. The teacher shows surprised interest and even pleasure in the boy's inventiveness. She asks how he got the idea and compliments him for thinking of drawing the inside of the head instead of the outside. She discusses with him what parts go where and asks him if he thinks he could improve his drawing. She suggests that he have a look at the health chart in the library, because they have some drawings of teeth there. She later asks the rest of the class if anyone else drew the inside of a head or thought of any other unusual way of doing it, and mentions that one boy did a good drawing showing the inside. She holds up his drawing, and the children admire it. As a result, the particular boy feels proud and pleased.

By considering how he could improve his drawing, he began to develop self-evaluation. He was encouraged to try to bring outside ideas into the classroom and to link up apparently totally different aspects of his experience. The other children saw how the teacher rewarded free-ranging thinking and were encouraged to try to do some themselves. A further example of the way in which a teacher can "open" the classroom for creativity, even with an unpromising group of students, is given in the following case study.

Our grade nine teacher of English was called Mr. Thompson. He really was an inspiration to us students. He was always coming up with new ideas. He was a real bundle of energy. You can imagine what a class of boys thought of English, and particularly of poetry, as a subject for discussion and study! But Mr. Thompson got us to the point where we were writing our own poems by the score. Not only that, but we proudly read them to each other and didn't feel like a bunch of fools. The school newspaper that year was half full of poems from our class.

How did he do it? Well, it was easy, really. He started talking to us about interesting experiences he had had, like going to the track and watching the stock car races. We didn't mind talking about that sort of thing—what did it have to do with English, anyway? One day he held us spellbound while he roared and swayed at the front of the room, describing a race he had watched. He made the sounds, steered around the bends, slammed his foot on the brake at the curve, and brought it all to life for us.

Then he really gave us a surprise. Just before the end of the lesson, he pulled out a piece of paper and read us a poem he had written himself in which he described the race he had just talked about. That took up the rest of the time. Next poetry lesson he talked about his poem. He showed us that using poetry gave him special ways of describing the scene that prose didn't encourage. We then told him about exciting things we had seen ourselves, and he invited us to write poems about them and read them in class. Some of them weren't much, but we all improved, and soon we were writing like mad, prose and poetry, with the result that I've already mentioned for the school newspaper.

Many teachers may lack Mr. Thompson's ability to act vividly scenes that would interest 14-year-old boys, or to write exciting descriptions of them. However, some general principles for encouraging creativity can be recognized in his handling of poetry lessons. Analyze his behavior and the students' responses from the point of view of fostering creativity.

FURTHER READING

Bloomberg, M. (Ed.). (1973). *Creativity: Theory and research.* New Haven, CT: College and University Press.

Getzels, N. W., & Csikszentmihalyi M. (1976). *The creative vision: A longitudinal study of problem solving in art.* New York: Wiley.

Khatena, J. (1984). *Imagery and creative imagination.* Buffalo, NY: Bearly.

Mansfield, R. J., & Busse, T. V. (1981). *The psychology of creativity and discovery.* Chicago: Nelson Hall.

Runco, M. A., & Albert, R. S. (Eds.). (1990). *Theories of creativity.* Newbury Park, CA: Sage.

Stanley, J. C., George, W. C., & H. C. Solano (Eds.). (1977). *The gifted and the creative.* Baltimore: Johns Hopkins University Press.

Vernon, P. E. (Ed.). (1970). *Creativity.* Harmondsworth, UK: Penguin.

5

Social and Emotional Blocks to Creative Thinking

BLOCKS WITHIN THE SOCIETY

The Effects of Socialization

Human newborns display many socially unacceptable behaviors. However, with the passage of time hitherto asocial infants come more and more to display patterns of behavior regarded as correct and even laudable by those around them. They may even reach a point at which they frown upon those who fail to obey the social standards, and take pride and pleasure in keeping to the culture's notions of what is proper and what improper. This is scarcely surprising, as there are definite payoffs for limiting behavior in keeping with the culture's demands. Punishment and social censure attach to proscribed behavior, reward and approbation to socially acceptable behavior. In fact, a major aspect of intellectual development is the acquisition of the culture's accumulated lore and wisdom, through the process of *socialization.*

Socialization involves training children, and adults too, to behave in ways that are valued by the society into which they are being socialized. Thus, one of its major effects is to stabilize behavior in well-socialized individuals and to reduce the range and variety of behaviors they emit. Subsequently, those who have been socialized grow up and become, in their turn, the socializers. This results in a great deal of similarity in the kinds of behavior demonstrated by adult models, and subsequently of behaviors which are rewarded during the socialization of the next generation of children. There is also great similarity in the kinds of behavior that are suppressed, because they are never demonstrated or are punished or ignored if they do occur. As Fromm (1980) put it, society has "filters" through which behavior, or even ideas, must pass: Deviance is filtered out.

It would be incorrect to suggest that socialization dictates exactly how a given person should behave in a particular situation. Nonetheless it is apparent that, in a given culture, a socially stereotyped band of highly desirable behaviors exists, along with a penumbra of tolerable behaviors, and finally a shadow area of undesirable ill-mannered or even proscribed behavior. Individuals are normally subjected to pressure to emit only behavior which lies within the tolerated limits of their societies, and suffer various punishments if their behavior falls into the shadow zone. Acceptance of the norms is advantageous for the individual: It facilitates comfortable living with other people, makes communication easy, and fosters a sense of belongingness. The key effect as far as the present book is concerned, however, is that the range of behaviors normally seen in individual members of a particular cultural group is restricted, with behaviors lying outside the limits being proscribed or at least discouraged. In a certain sense, then, the acquisition of a culture's modus operandi restricts variety in behavior.

Studies of creative mathematicians, scientists, architects, writers, and business managers have shown that, in addition to being flexible, curious, and original, they are individualistic, nonconforming, unsociable, low in impulse control, independent, and willing to take risks (see pp. 17ff.). Creative people have also been described as self-actualized, dependent upon feelings rather than judgments, and inner rather than outer directed (Maslow, 1971; Houtz, Jambor, Cifone, & Lewis, 1989). From the psychoanalytic viewpoint, they are able to express drives in more direct, undisguised forms, whereas in the average individual drive content is modified in accordance with social dictates, and impulses are expressed in socially acceptable forms. Thus, descriptions of the personalities of creative people emphasize that they show low levels of conformity to the standard style of relating to their environments, depending more upon their own internal feelings to guide them than on social precepts, and expressing their own impulses in less socially stereotyped forms than do noncreative people.

Both the intellectual processes of creative people and their personality structures thus involve a great deal of deviation from societal norms of behavior, to the point where social nonconformity is their most visible social characteristic. It is often so prominent that some observers confuse it with creativity itself. Creative people go beyond the limits of socially approved behavior for their cultures and penetrate the shadowy areas. Not only do they think thoughts which lie beyond the realm of their culture's commonplace, and which venture into the surprising or even shocking, but their own idiosyncratic organizations of reactions to the external world (their personalities) are so "poorly" socialized as to make them individualistic, bold, unconventional, and willing to tolerate a great deal of uncertainty. All of this means that they represent a kind of "failure" of the standardizing and homogenizing socialization processes which have already been discussed. Indeed, particular societies' responses to some creators indicate that censure, ridicule, and even imprisonment are sometimes the lot of the creative individual (see Cropley, 1973, for a more detailed discussion).

This section may be summarized by saying that creativity can be conceptualized as a social phenomenon, with the creative person being distinguished by a disposition to behave in what are essentially poorly socialized ways. Despite their obvious and real utility, socialization processes thus have anticreative side effects, in that extremely clear-cut, strongly enforced societal norms militate against the appearance of widely divergent behaviors in a culture, and hence against creativity. A major aspect of creative individuals is, therefore, their ability to extend the limits of their culture's thinking about how the world is organized, and to find solutions to problems even though they may have to go beyond the limits their culture's socialization processes normally impose. An important social function of creative people is thus that of updating, extending, and broadening a culture's values, norms, and lifeways.

Blocks Within the Society and the Classroom

The factors inhibiting creativity thus lie partly within the social structure. Building on ideas developed by Torrance (1963), social blocks can be summarized as follows:

Success Orientation. Clearly, being successful is a pleasant experience. Furthermore, there are personal rewards to be obtained from success, such as a feeling of satisfaction. There are also rewards for the society in having people who can solve problems. However, excessive emphasis on success sets up a major block to creative thinking in schoolchildren. It may lead to overemphasis on acquisition of all the facts, on detailed prior planning, on avoidance of unexpected difficulties or problems, and on one-sided insistence on correctness. Although success is a desirable goal, it is important that it does not become so important that it forces thinking into a narrow straitjacket.

Sanctions against Questioning. Related both to the success orientation and to other pressures to complete specified workloads is the problem of sanctions imposed against curiosity and marginally relevant issues. The child who asks questions which do not seem to bear directly on the matter at hand is likely to be strongly discouraged and told not to waste time. This is particularly true if the questions asked are unexpected or obscure, in the judgment of the teacher. The teacher is normally operating within a convergent system, and has the additional problem of looking after the needs of children other than the one who has asked an annoying question. Sanctions against asking questions need not be the result of maliciousness or stupidity on the part of teachers but may simply reflect the pressures of work in the classroom.

External Evaluation. One of these pressures is that all participants in the classroom process are likely to be subject to external evaluation. For the teacher, this probably takes the form of a requirement that a certain syllabus be covered during the year, that students be prepared for examinations which demonstrate the extent to which such coverage has been achieved, and that advancement in the profession depends upon performance. Teachers may, with some justification, regard the criterion of their performance as lying somewhere beyond the classroom in "the system." It is true that, in many countries, *formal* pressures of this kind have now been greatly reduced, especially in elementary schools. However, teachers are still responsible to the community, which may continue to impose informal or unofficial standards, even when the official ones have been relaxed. There is evidence of an increasingly strong "back to basics" movement, both officially and unofficially. This movement is by no means incompatible with the suggestions in the present book but may lead to excessive emphasis on external criteria. For the pupil, the major source of external evaluation is likely to be the teacher, although the teacher's own judgments will reflect other external pressures. There is, then, a serious danger that children will come to regard the approbation of authorities external to themselves (especially their teachers) as being the sole criterion of the worthwhileness of their ideas. Such an attitude is clearly not at all favorable to intrinsic motivation, nor to production of ideas. Amabile et al. (1990) stated the case against extrinsic motivation unusually strongly and concluded that it is incompatible with creativity.

This does not mean that external evaluation can be totally ignored. On the contrary, it is clear that some interest in the relationship between one's own behavior and other people's ideas is always desirable. The problem is that external criteria, which are often useful or even necessary, tend to assume the role of invariant, ironclad rules which continue to be applied even when the need for them no longer exists.

Conformity Pressure. An outstanding feature of children's behavior is a pronounced tendency to conform to peer pressures. Ironically, one way of conforming is even to be a stereotyped nonconformist! Conformity is seen in such concrete matters as styles of dress and hair length, and is also seen in the social domain. For example, in some subcultures it would be highly embarrassing for a boy at a certain age to sit next to a girl. Children's behavior toward each other, towards the teacher, and towards classroom learning becomes highly stereotyped. Standardization of behavior may also be encouraged by teachers who insist on absolutely uniform format for written work and standardized approaches to various situations. One result of this is that children frequently go to considerable lengths to disguise their differences from their peers. The child who expresses unusual ideas, establishes an atypical relationship with the teacher, or displays nonstandard attitudes towards learning may be subjected to very strong peer pressures to conform. Many children may become afraid to express their ideas until they have first ascertained that they are run-of-the-mill and conventional, for fear of being ridiculed or socially rejected (Freeman, 1983; Kerry, 1981). These authors discussed in some detail the role of such peer pressure in inhibiting creativity: One result can be that children deliberately hide their ideas in order to seem just like the others.

Strict Sex Roles. One aspect of the conformity pressures just discussed is the insistence that children play highly stereotyped sex roles; the stereotypical male role is well known, as is the stereotypical female role— the reference here is to traditional stereotypes, which may be changing in the light of changing community attitudes to the sexes. Conformity to these roles is demanded both by peers and by many teachers and parents. However, psychological research has shown that highly creative males tend to possess above-average levels of stereotypically feminine traits. The reverse is true for highly creative females (see, for instance, Hammer, 1964, and Helson, 1966). In other words, one feature of creative people appears to be their ability to function in ways which do not conform to the stereotype for their sex. Highly creative girls display marked levels of ambitiousness, determination, and toughness of mind. On the other hand, highly creative boys show marked levels of aesthetic feeling, intuitiveness, and sensitivity for other people's feelings. The special characteristic of highly creative people is that they are able to fuse the feminine and masculine sides of their personalities. Consequently, strict adherence to conventional sex role stereotypes looks to be antithetical to creativity, although it is not clear whether this is because cross-sex characteristics are themselves helpful in creativity, or because persons who resist rigid sex role stereotyping also resist the other conformity pressure that have already been discussed.

Equating Difference with Abnormality. Society in general, and schoolchildren in particular, tend to regard the unusual, individualistic, or different person as being in some way weird or sick. One example of this (see Torrance, 1965) was a boy of very high IQ who was consistently reported by his teachers to be mentally disturbed. When tested by school psychologists, he was invariably found to be a brilliant boy. However, he could not function in the ordinary classroom setting, because he did not conform to the existing pressures. As a result, he was labelled "mentally defective" and eventually found his way into a remedial class for retarded children. In this particular case, the problem was not one of low level of ability at all, but of differentness that had been labelled defectiveness.

Distinction between Work and Play. A final block to creativity involves the strict sanctions against play that are imposed in most classrooms. Work is regarded as something that is done in silence and with grim concentration. Play is regarded as something that goes on outside the classroom, is probably noisy, and, most important of all, never yields worthwhile results except of a recreational nature. Consequently, any looseness of associations, introduction of tangential ideas in an attempt to find a solution to a problem, humor, noisiness, or even show of enjoyment is highly suspect in a situation which has been defined as work. The idea that a problem could be solved by playing with it is rejected, and the fresh insights that can be obtained in this way are lost.

Two case studies based on press reports illustrate some of the points just outlined as they can operate in practice. The first is taken from an article in *Time* (April 23, 1979). Tommy was regarded by his teachers as a problem child virtually from his first day at school: He had difficulty in concentrating, disturbed the other children, and did poorly in tests. When he reached the third grade, his parents were advised that he was suffering from a learning disability. This surprised them: from the age of 4 Tommy was able to defeat all comers at chess and knew the names of all the organs of the human body, to give only two examples of his capacities. The parents had him tested by an independent psychologist who determined that he had an IQ of 170, a score placing him in the genius capacity rather than the learning disabled! The second study concerns a Swedish boy who suffered a similar fate (published in *Die Zeit,* December 12, 1971). When he began school, he could not only defeat local adults at chess, but already spoke five languages fluently. He could hardly wait to start school, and set off on the first few mornings with high enthusiasm. However, problems arose at once: in particular, he could not fit in. At first he tried to act just like the others, but he soon became isolated and began to avoid contact to other children and teachers, and then began to attempt to avoid school itself by faking illnesses. As in the American case, a psychological examination revealed that the boy had an IQ of 170!

The problem with both boys was not that they were unintelligent or against school—quite the contrary—but that they were too full of ideas, too demanding, and too excited about the opportunities offered by school. McLeod and Cropley (1989) summarized the situation in a bitter joke: A schoolgirl is almost leaping out of her seat in her eagerness to answer a teacher's question; the teacher glares at her and says, "Sit down, Mary, and be stupid like the rest!"

BLOCKS WITHIN THE INDIVIDUAL

Just as it is possible to describe a number of classroom or societal conditions which inhibit creative thinking in school children, it is also possible to identify attitudes and values within each individual child that may impede creative thinking. Once again building on Torrance (1963), it can be said that these intrapersonal blocks to creativity include:

Inability to "let go". As a result of a self-imposed discipline that controls ideas, especially those which are unusual, playful, unexpected, or marginally relevant, the child may reach a point at which it becomes very difficult to release the imagination and let ideas flow. A kind of mental constipation occurs. Using a different metaphor, Hare (1982) called for the "unfreezing" of ideas.

Fear of letting the imagination loose. Children may actually fear freeing their imaginations, especially in the presence of others, in case this should involve them in punishments either tangible or intangible. The child who gives an offbeat, unexpected, or disconcerting answer to a teacher may be punished for doing so. Even if no punishment ensues, the child may be subjected to the kinds of social sanction discussed earlier. It may be considerably less threatening to deliver what is expected, rather than to use personal divergent thinking capacities.

Preference for analytical thinking. The kinds of problems conventionally posed in the classroom tend to require analytical rather than synthetic thinking. The child who does not want to experience social sanctions, and who wishes to give correct responses, will find that it is far more advantageous to think analytically rather than synthetically. The result may eventually be that divergent thinking becomes difficult or is habitually avoided.

Premature closure. Where correct answers are required as fast as possible through the application of convergent thinking, a strong tendency to seize upon an obvious and readily obtainable answer may develop. As a result, the child may acquire the habit of cutting off thinking about a problem as soon as the first acceptable solution is achieved, regardless of whether this solution is the best, or even a particularly good one.

Persistence of set. When a problem has been successfully solved by the application of a particular thinking process, there is a strong tendency for the successful strategy to be repeated. In other words, what worked in the past is assumed to be likely to work again in the future. This is the phenomenon of "set" in thinking processes. When a set becomes unduly persistent, a child may apply it again and again, especially if it permits early closure and so earns some degree of reward from external authorities. Persisting along a single track may thus, although being moderately useful, inhibit a child from imaginative or creative solutions.

Inability to handle ideas. The control of ideas, which may flow in large numbers when the divergent thinking floodgate is opened, is itself a problem. A child who is inexperienced in coping with a large number of ideas may find this unpleasant or frightening, especially where there is strong pressure for closure and consequent fear of letting oneself go.

At a party some years ago in Australia I was asked by the hosts, who knew of my interest in creativity, to say which of their two sons was more creative. According to them, one was highly creative, the other not at all. I asked the first boy (in the absence of his brother) to suggest some interesting and unusual ways of using a tin can. He replied after some hesitation with suggestions such as "saucepan," "bucket," or "flowerpot"— not foolish, but decidedly everyday. I then asked the other boy the same question. He asked me if I really wanted unusual uses, and, when I said I did, he began to generate answers at a great pace; a single example will illustrate the quality of his suggestions—"put four holes in the can at opposite corners, put a mouse inside with its legs sticking out of these holes and solder on the lid (leave a hole for the mouse's head to stick out). Bring in the family cat and witness the first-ever fair fight between cat and mouse!" After 10 minutes the parents told their son to go to bed, but he had to be dragged upstairs, still shouting new ideas. The party resumed, but, after half an hour, one of the windows suddenly flew open and the boy jumped inside—he had climbed out of his bedroom window, down the drainpipe, and established from the voices where I was sitting. He rushed up to me and shouted out, "Cut teeth in the bottom and jam it in the chimney as a Santa Claus trap—you could help yourself to all the presents in his sack!" The parents were embarrassed, and once again he was hustled upstairs, this time with the aid of several slaps on the backside! This boy had certainly lost control of the flow of ideas and could not wait to tell someone—as the spanking showed, this can be a dangerous business.

Anxiety. When confronted by excessively close external evaluation, very high goals and fear of criticism, a child's classroom experience may be marked by high levels of anxiety. Such anxiety has the effect of increasing fear of letting oneself go, encouraging premature closure, and fostering rigid dependence on an existing set. Finally, the number of alternative ideas that can be handled decreases sharply under conditions of high anxiety. Thus, excessive worry in the classroom leads to stereotyped, rigid, and inflexible thinking and is not at all conducive to creative thinking.

Excessive emphasis on verbal expression. Cutting across these intrapersonal blocks to creativity is the custom of regarding words as the only proper way in which to express ideas. Children who have difficulty in expressing themselves verbally are thus placed at a considerable disadvantage. Creative ideas which do not lend themselves readily to verbal expression may have to be completely suppressed, in the absence of acceptance of any alternative modes of expression.

Possible alternative, nonverbal methods of expressing ideas can, however, be used. Ideas may be expressed graphically through the use of drawings, through the construction of models, and through other modes such as movement (dance, calisthenics, or gymnastics). There is still overwhelming emphasis in the classroom on verbal expression of ideas, and many children will prefer this mode. However, a failure to recognize any other ways of expressing ideas means that the possibilities for some children to express themselves are unnecessarily restricted.

CASE STUDIES

Here is an example of the way in which teachers may establish either a negative or a positive climate for innovative, questioning behavior.

The scene is a class of 12-year-olds in the science laboratory. The teacher is demonstrating an experiment at the front bench. He applies a match to the bottom of a flask filled with water and fitted with a stopper and glass tubing which projects vertically. The water (colored so that it can be seen easily) slowly rises up the tubing from its original level, which has been marked on the outside of the tube. The teacher then removes the match, and the water returns to its original level in the tube. Next, he heats the flask with a bunsen burner and the water rises rapidly up the tube, reaching a higher level than that reached when the match was used to provide the heat. The teacher points out that this demonstrates expansion of the water on being heated, and contraction on subsequent cooling. He then asks the class what would happen if he applied a really hot flame such as that from an oxyacetylene torch. One child interrupts by asking if the water would shrink if he applied a cold flame.

Blocking response—The rest of the class lets out sniggers and groans. A voice is heard to mutter: "Shut up, Green, you're always asking dumb questions!" The teacher puts on an air of amazement and then resigned patience. With the manner of one speaking to a halfwit, he slowly and distinctly exclaims: "A flame can't be cold. It has to be hot enough for the substance to burn. You know, B, U, R, N—burn! Would you like to come up to the front here and stick your hand in the flame to prove it?" (He speaks with great patience and noble long-suffering.) "Now just copy your notes from the board and don't waste our time with any more of this sort of rubbish!" The teacher then returns to his lesson, introducing his remarks with: "As I was saying, before I was interrupted by Mr. Green." He glares at the offender, now totally demoralized, and goes on with a clear, informative, and valuable account of the effects of heat and cold on fluids, ultimately explaining the principle of the thermometer. The facts are well presented, as he is a dedicated and skillful teacher.

Unfortunately, the student named Green and the other students were all taught a lesson about the danger of asking questions. This is especially true when ideas for questions come from outside the classroom or even from outside the school. The sarcastic reaction of the teacher indicated rejection of the question-asking student and even implied that such behavior is a sign of mental deficiency (equating difference with abnormality). It fostered feelings of anxiety in students with ideas and delivered a telling blow in the development of a classroom atmosphere antagonistic to divergence and originality.

Opening response—The teacher responds by asking: "All right, what would happen if the flame were cold?" Cries go up from other students that this is impossible. However, the teacher insists that it is a good question, treats it at face value, and insists that the class work out the answer—the water will be cooled, and will contract down the tube. He then goes on to ask whether it would be possible to have a cold flame. Subsequently, he introduces information concerning the effects of pressure on boiling points and the idea of cold boiling. The students are given a riddle to solve for homework. "Why do they drink weak tea on the top of Mount Everest?"[1]

The unexpected question can therefore be used as the jumping-off point for a worthwhile lesson, instead of being rejected as stupid or time wasting. The class might see the teacher actually show interest in a point initiated from one of its members. Divergent questioners could be encouraged to incorporate ideas from another sphere into their thinking, and be given positive reinforcement for question asking. The question can be treated seriously, and the child's idea valued. Teachers can themselves display originality and ingenuity in following up the lesson with a divergent assignment.

Punishment for getting deeply involved—This happened to me when I was 13. It was in a German lesson in high school. Our teacher had read the poem "Die Lorelei" with us in class. For homework, we had to learn it by heart. I was very keen on German and made up my mind to learn it really well. After school, I happened to speak to a neighbor who was a migrant from

---

[1] Because water boils at too low a temperature to brew strong tea, as a result of the low atmospheric pressure 29,000 feet above sea level.

Germany. She told me that the poem, which I had started to recite to her for practice (I had learned it already on the bus on the way home from school), had been set to music. She then sang it to me. Suddenly I had an idea. I would learn the tune and sing the poem in class next day! I got busy and mastered the tune, singing the whole poem through a few times until I had words and music clear in my mind.

At school next day I waited eagerly for German. I was hoping that the teacher would ask me to recite the poem. I got more and more impatient as the time passed until at least it was time for German. Imagine being excited at the prospect of being tested on homework! We got ready for the lesson, the teacher announced that she was going to go over the homework, and I prayed that she would choose me. I must have looked particularly eager, because the big moment arrived—she did pick me to recite. My heart gave a lurch of excitement—I knew that I had prepared better than any of the others, and that I would be a sensation! I opened my mouth, and nothing came out. My mind was a total blank!

I struggled to remember the poem in the awful few seconds that followed my name being called. Then the fog cleared, and the opening words and bars began to come into focus. I took a breath before speaking, but at that moment the teacher started on me. She screeched abuse at me, telling me that I was a lazy good-for-nothing, and that she was fed up with me and people like me who did not do their homework. She made me stay in after school and write out the poem 10 times. She was punishing me for trying too hard. I got personally involved in the work and got too excited about it. I was bursting with ideas and enthusiasm, and that was my problem. If only I had just half learned the poem and had the first few words written on my wrist. Everything would have been all right then. I hope she reads this and feels ashamed of herself, but I don't suppose she will.

Why would a teacher behave in this way? Should the teacher refrain from ever showing annoyance or dissatisfaction for fear of repeating the misunderstanding described in the case study? How could the teacher have avoided the present student's resentment and disappointment, and even rewarded the deep involvement, while still making it plain that homework has to be done if a foreign language is to be mastered?

Alternative modes of expression—When I was in grade 5 we had a teacher for English who always tried to think up new and interesting ways of doing things. One day we read a story about a prince who got lost and had to find his way back to his father's kingdom. After we had read the story the teacher asked us how we would have got on if we had been in the prince's position. We all thought that it would be easy for a prince, but the teacher asked us if we thought a prince who had lived all his life in a castle would be good at finding his way around the world of the common people. It would be no good telling them that he was the prince, as they would never believe him. As the teacher put it, it would be almost as though the boy could not talk to anyone.

Some of us still said that it would be easy for a prince, so the teacher told us that he would help us to feel what it might be like. He told me that I could pick three or four other boys as my helpers, and that our job would be to act out the problem without speaking. Some of us would be people from the country, and I was the prince. We were sent out to the boys' shelter shed to practice for half an hour (he must have picked children who were ahead in their other work, I suppose), and we had to make up and rehearse a mime. Eventually he sent another boy to call us in, and we had to perform. We all tried to get the feel of being lost and not allowed to talk, and we tried to show our ideas by the ways we moved our bodies and the looks on our faces. We waved our arms to indicate emotions. We screwed up our faces to show that we were asking questions. We shrugged, bobbed, and nodded. Still, we must have got the message over, as the other kids seemed to enjoy it.

What extension to children's idea getting and expressing capacities was being fostered by this teacher? What straitjacket on broad-ranging and adventurous thinking was he helping to remove? Apart from the content of the play itself, what skills would the children be encouraged to learn?

Making a person with a difference feel abnormal—I recall being in grade1, and being left-handed, and automatically starting to print from the right-hand side of the page towards the left. This was quickly and abruptly corrected by being told that it was the wrong way; everybody does it the other way. I, of course, switched to the "right" way and got my printing assignments back marked "messy" or "does not try to be neat." She could not believe that I was doing the best I could and that I wanted to write as well as the "normal" children who were right-handed. The result in me was not knowing how to be correct and feeling anxious; this persisted until I adjusted to being a passable, sloppy, left-handed person. But it was touch and go. If I had been a bit more anxious and a bit less tough, I would have finished up with a lot of anxieties about my difference from the "good" children.

The girl who describes her problem in this case study was different only because she was left-handed. Generalize and extend the situation to take in children who find that their ideas are treated as weird or crazy, that their solutions to problems are regarded as bizarre, and that their conversation is unintelligible to their classmates and teachers. On the other hand, it is useful to be able to write intelligibly and to communicate with other people in terms they can understand. How can this tension between acceptance of difference and preservation of relations with the average, normal, or conventional be handled by teachers?

Allowing work and play to exist side by side—In a first-year high school Geometry class the teacher is revising the facts about figures with straight lines as sides. She draws various figures on the board and asks the members of the class to identify them by name. The children respond by calling out in unison "triangle" when she points to a three-sided figure, "rectangle" for the appropriate figure, "hexagon," and "octagon." She asks if anyone can tell her a single word which refers to any closed figure with straight lines as sides, but no one can give the name she is seeking. Finally, she provides it herself, telling the students that the name for any such figure is "polygon." She then points to the triangle and says: "This is a polygon!" She points to the rectangle, "This is a polygon," to the hectagon, "and this is a polygon," and then continues for each figure on the blackboard.

She asks the class, "Do you all know now what a polygon is? Let's see if everyone does know. Smith, come out to the board and draw a polygon for us." The boy does so. He draws a square. "Yes, a square is a kind of polygon. Now someone else..." Two or three children draw figures on the board. It is now the turn of Davis, a notorious nuisance. He keeps putting up his hand until the teacher can no longer resist giving him his turn at the board. Davis goes to the front of the class and engages himself busily for some time. He then steps back to reveal a crude sketch of a parrot hanging upside down from its perch by its chain. The teacher demands: "What on earth is that, for Heaven's sake? I asked you to draw a polygon." The boy replies with a broad grin: "That's what it is, miss. It's a dead parrot—a polly gone!" The class gapes in silence for a few moments, then the ones quicker on the uptake burst out laughing.

What should the teacher do? Given what was presented in this chapter, what risks are inherent in the situation, as far as maintenance of a productive teaching and learning atmosphere are concerned? How can the teacher use this episode as a jumping-off point in order to open up the classroom for creativity?

> *External evaluation*—An advanced English class has been studying the poem "Christabel." The atmosphere of strangeness and unnaturalness has been emphasized by the teacher. She has pointed out that this is typical of Coleridge's poems. The lesson turns to the techniques through which the poet achieves his effects, and the teacher reads out several passages. She then asks how these passages make students feel and how it is that this feeling is achieved. One girl tries to describe the sense of eeriness and supernatural strangeness created in her by the poet's words. The teacher listens patiently and then says: "No, that wasn't the answer I wanted. Who else would like to try?"

The student concerned was a keen English student. However, she never forgave this teacher for this episode. Why? What attitude towards their own feelings and emotions would the teacher's behavior be likely to foster in students? In what sense is the behavior a blocking response? How could a teacher elicit the particular comment she was seeking (whatever it was) from the class in such a way as to open the lesson to creativity?

FURTHER READING

Bruner, J. S. (1962). The conditions of creativity. In H. Gruber, G. Terrell, & M. Wertheimer (Eds.), *Contemporary approaches to creative thinking.* New York: Atherton Press.

Feldhusen, J. F., & Treffinger, D. J. (1980). *Creating thinking and problem solving in gifted education.* Dubuque, IA: Kendall/Hunt.

Hare, A. P. (1982). *Creativity in small groups.* Beverly Hills, CA: Sage.

Mooney, R., & Razik, T. (Eds.). (1967). *Explorations in creativity.* New York: Harper & Row (see especially the chapters by A. H. Maslow, C. McGuire, and P. S. Weisberg and K. J. Springer).

Wall, W. D. (1976). *Constructive education for children.* London: Harrap.

6

The Role of the Teacher in Fostering Creativity

Zajonc (1965) argued that there are three basic modes through which people influence other people's behavior: by modeling behavior, by "energizing" learning, and finally by administering differential reinforcement to successive approximations of the required behavior. All three of these modes of influence are available to the teacher, as will been shown in this chapter. The first mode of action centers on the teacher as a model; teachers can influence students' behavior through the kinds of behavior they themselves display. The second mode of action involves the "climate" or "atmosphere" in the classroom; when this is favorable, creativity is energized. The third is to be found in the specific patterns of reward and punishment offered, the kinds of behaviors that are encouraged, and the activities for which opportunities are provided.

The Creative Teacher

Children learn rapidly from the observation of models provided by prestigious adults. Thus, despite the kinds of thing that they tell their students to do, teachers find that students also learn by observing their teachers. The old saying "Do as I say, not as I do" is quite inconsistent with the ways in which children really do learn. Empirical studies have shown that there is a direct relationship between the degree to which teachers display behavior typical of divergent thinkers (even if they are not aware of this in any formal way), and the extent to which the pupils themselves exhibit divergent thinking. Similarly, many highly divergent children perform best in classrooms with highly divergent teachers, even though both teachers and students may be unaware of specific methods of encouraging divergent thinking (Cropley, 1967a). Finally, it has also been shown that teachers who have more knowledge of divergent thinking and associated concepts subsequently permit higher levels of creativity in their students, even if they make no special and conscious effort to encourage it. Patterning or modeling of creative behavior on the part of a teacher, then, is a potent factor in fostering creativity in students. Among others, Torrance (1965) demonstrated that a positive attitude to creativity among teachers fosters creativity in pupils.

Many teachers are aware of the need for a more creative approach on their own part. Just as it is difficult among schoolchildren to distinguish between creativity and mere nonconformity or sterile refusal to defer to authority, it is easy for teachers to mistake the superficial trappings of nonconformity for creativity. Adoption of a stylized manner of "creative" dress and personal grooming may or may not be associated with creative attitudes and habits in teachers. Carried to extremes, it may have the reverse of the desired effects, as the following example shows.

The scene. A school psychologist is interviewing a 12-year-old boy who has been skipping school. The boy's teacher is a young man of very "advanced" personal style. He wears bell-bottom jeans and a cheesecloth shirt, with beads, headband, and peace symbols. He has long hair and a thick, untrimmed beard. The psychologist knows that the teacher is an intelligent, concerned, and sensible young man, and is puzzled that he has not been able to influence the boy's behavior more, at least to the point where open rebellion and consequent punishment are no longer common. He asks the boy about the teacher: "What about Mr. Graham? Haven't you talked it over with him?" The boy's reply is devastating. "Mr. Graham? Oh, you mean 'The Hippy'—we all call him that. He's neat, but we don't take any notice of what he says. He's just a hippy!"

In actual fact, the boy's assessment of the teacher was quite wrong. Mr. Graham had much to offer. He was relaxed and informal with his students, but by adopting the superficial trappings of creativity, he had sacrificed his credibility with them. It would have been much more perceptive of him to have discerned this particular group's need for a teacher with certain airs of adult authority and to have adjusted his external image accordingly.

Despite Mr. Graham's experience, some degree of identification with the concerns of students can be achieved, with results beneficial to the development of divergent thinking. For example, students in a high school resented the school dress regulations, and one girl actually announced that she would not obey them any more. A confrontation with the school authorities loomed, with probable bitterness on both sides. However, the social studies teacher discussed the issue in class on the day matters threatened to come to a head. She maintained that it was hard to believe that the rules about dress were merely capricious or malicious, and that there might be some rational basis to them. She pointed out that, even in the one class, there was a difference of opinion on the question. Finally, she asked the girl leading the rebellion to supervise a survey of student and parent opinion on the matter, as a class project. The goal of this survey was to prepare a summary of views both for and against dress regulations, and to analyze their strengths and weaknesses. The upshot of it all was some relaxation in the rules, avoidance of a confrontation, and a great deal of student insight into the whole matter of opinion sampling and the sociology of school uniforms.

In a similar vein, a teacher confronted with a class who complained that his History class was not "relevant" accepted their criticism and asked them to design a relevant class that would still meet the curriculum requirements. The teacher showed that he was sympathetic to the students' views, interested in their opinions, and capable of changing his behavior. He demonstrated his own ability to be innovative and flexible, and he offered a positive climate for the advancement of ideas. The students carried out an extensive survey of the historical period involved and made many interesting discoveries about the universalities of human behavior. Thus, it is not necessary for creative teachers to identify with established authority at all times. Nor need they be distinguished merely by the adoption of stylized "creative" traits.

Methods of encouraging creativity in school children may be understood better by considering the behavior which characterizes creative teachers. A number of studies have attempted to isolate some of the definitive characteristics of the creative teacher, and considerable agreement has been reached among them. McLeod and Cropley (1989) summarized findings concerning creative teachers. They are:

- inclined to be flexible and willing to "get off the beaten track";
- resourceful in introducing new materials and in finding ways to present knowledge to children;
- capable of enjoying good relations with all of their students but inclined to have particularly good relations with highly divergent children. This feature of the creative teacher is in direct contrast to the usual relationship between teachers and divergent-thinking pupils;
- likely to be nonconforming and even critical and fault finding in their relationships with their colleagues;
- self-critical and frequently dissatisfied with themselves and the system in which they are operating.

Establishing a Creative Classroom Atmosphere

Williams (1976a, b, c), Hare (1982), and Treffinger et al. (1983) emphasized that creativity in the classroom requires, not only knowledge and ability, but also motivation and a classroom climate that fosters confidence and daring. Teachers exercise influence through the atmosphere or climate they establish. As one writer in the area has put it (although writing about "inquiry learning" rather than specifically creativity), the emergence of creative learning in the classroom requires, in addition to the capacity to produce ideas (i.e., in addition to the intellectual basis of creativity), several emotional and motivational conditions. These include a desire within the individual to function creatively. Of even greater relevance to the present context, creativity requires a setting in which there is freedom to have and express ideas, along with an environment that is constructively responsive to new ideas and in which the creative child can evaluate them free of fear of rejection or ridicule. In this description of the creativity-fostering classroom, it is clear that an atmosphere or climate that is not only intellectual, but also emotional and motivational, is conceptualized. A class may function in a climate ranging from confident to anxious. Morale may range from high to low. The teacher may be a dominant figure or a nonentity. These kinds of variables determine "classroom climate." This mood or spirit of the classroom is, of course, important to all children. However, in view of the potential blocks to creativity, the classroom's social and intellectual climate is of particular importance to the highly divergent student.

The teacher can help to remove blocks to creativity by establishing a climate in which children may express themselves freely. *Intrapersonal conditions* favorable to the manifestation of creative thinking are fostered when the teacher helps the children to understand their own divergence and to esteem it highly, even in the presence of social pressures to the contrary. *Emotional conditions* for the emergence of creativity are fostered when the teacher encourages students to be aware of, and to respect, their own feelings. In the same way, a favorable *motivational climate* for divergent thinking is facilitated when anxiety is reduced through the elimination of a general sense of threat in the classroom. However, motivation for creativity does require that children become aware of gaps in knowledge and discrepancies between areas of knowledge. It also requires a climate in which there can be constructive criticism and informative feedback.

In view of the possibility of peer group pressure or other social sanctions against particularly divergent children, it is often necessary for teachers to form a personal relationship with them to give them a sense of security and confidence. The teacher may become the creative child's sponsor, providing a kind of refuge for the child when pressure becomes too great. One way in which the teacher can do this is to help creative children in getting along with other people, that is, by fostering *interpersonal conditions* favorable to creative thinking. For example, the teacher may encourage creative pupils to present their own ideas, but to state them in terms relevant to other people's goals. Similarly, they can be encouraged to express their criticisms of other people's ideas in a constructive and positive way.

It is a help to divergent thinkers to earn a certain freedom from criticism by making concessions to the demands of the group. They can be encouraged to present themselves as supporting behaviors, opinions, and activities which command group respect. In a similar vein, creative children will find it helpful if they avoid threatening others and avoid destroying their dignity by making them look small or foolish. The child who can be persuaded by a teacher to make concessions of this kind is enabled, in fact, to "buy" a certain freedom from conformity pressure. It may also be necessary for teachers not only to help the peers of creative children, but also to assist their parents to understand the way in which their own children are different.

As far as classroom climate is concerned, then, the teacher's role is to overcome blocks to the emergence of divergent thinking by:

- eliminating negative sanctions against divergence;
- reducing anxiety about correctness or incorrectness;
- overcoming feelings of helplessness and friendlessness among the highly divergent;
- preventing ridicule or contempt from peers; and
- reducing misunderstanding and even despair on the part of the parents.

A favorable climate for creativity requires not only the elimination of negative elements or blocks, but also the provision of positive factors. These positive factors include:

- sensitivity to one's own feelings,
- interest in sensory experiences,
- openness to new ideas, and
- respect for the novel and unusual.

Sponsoring Creativity

A major element in the classroom is the teachers themselves. The often decisive role of an encouraging teacher in the development of children who later became famous has been demonstrated by Bloom (1985) in a series of retrospective case studies. In addition to the intrapersonal, motivational, and interpersonal atmosphere they foster, teachers can themselves promote or sponsor creativity. The role of the teacher in functioning as a sponsor of creativity, as well as tactics for helping creative children get along with their peers, are discussed in detail by Torrance (1962).

Teachers can do this through the activities in which they encourage students to participate, through the behaviors they reward most strongly, and through the opportunities for success they offer (Graham et al., 1989). It is important that teachers offer recognition and approval of divergent achievements. Such positive recognition also has the additional advantage of reducing negative reactions from classmates. Teachers can facilitate divergent thinking by giving students opportunities to communicate their ideas to others and by acknowledging divergent or creative ideas. This may involve responding to unusual questions with interest and respect rather than annoyance, and treating unusual ideas or solutions in a similar way. Teachers can also stress the value of ideas for solving problems. They may encourage the development of hypotheses as a source of ideas, even providing opportunities for "way-out" hunches as possible sources of a new approach to a problem. This may even extend to providing opportunities for students to "play" with problems, materials, and ideas, or to invoke fantasy as a legitimate source of ideas. This could be done, for example, by running a science fair exhibiting machines of the future, organizing a drama festival with a fantasy or futuristic theme, or having children write descriptions of historical events as they could have happened (but did not).

The Role of Evaluation

A vexed question concerns the role of evaluation in a classroom oriented towards developing creativity. Amabile et al. (1990) particularly emphasized the harmful effects on creativity of excessive dependence on external evaluation. The negative influence of anxiety, as well as of heavy reliance on external authorities, has suggested to some writers that evaluation should be totally abandoned. Certainly external evaluation and associated anxiety can be potent negative influences on divergent thinking. On the other hand, it is very difficult to believe that creativity involves the suspension of all judgment, or the unquestioning acceptance of any and all answers (Basadur, Wakabayashi, & Graen, 1990; Facaoaru, 1985; Runco, 1990). This becomes particularly clear when real life creativity is considered—scientific, technological, and engineering creators do not simply throw chemicals together or join up circuits at random. Facaoaru's (1985) study of creative engineers demonstrated the importance, not only of divergence, but also of conventional factors such as knowledge of facts. Even in the more subjective area of aesthetic creativity, painters, sculptors, and writers are all subject to a searching process of external evaluation.

Consequently, it does not seem reasonable to suggest that all evaluation is inimical to creativity. What is needed is not abandonment of any kind of evaluative process, but *a shift in the focus and locus of evaluation*.

The shift can be facilitated in two ways. Teachers can provide periods of nonevaluated activity in which ideas may be freely advanced, modified, and revised without risk of negative evaluation of any kind. They can also encourage delay in evaluation until an idea which may initially seem inappropriate has been pursued further. Teachers can help to shift the locus of evaluation from sources outside the child to sources within, without abandoning the idea that self-evaluation must still take account of the external world, by encouraging "guided self-evaluation" (Torrance, 1965). The notion here is that children need to evaluate their own efforts, but not purely in terms of whether these make them feel good. In guided self-evaluation, children decide how far their own ideas measure up to the demands of the external world, as well as being personally satisfying to them. The criterion, then, continues to be resident in the external world, but the major judge is the child. Such guided self-evaluation requires, of course, an appreciation of external criteria and a knowledge of the basic facts of a subject area. However, it emphasizes internal motives rather than the wishes of some external critic.

CASE STUDIES

The scene—The teacher has set a project on "Wheat Production in the Middle West" for an elementary school Social Studies class. She has collected and evaluated the reports and is now discussing them with each student. One boy has handed in a brief, inaccurate, untidy, and altogether unsatisfactory piece of work. The teacher is explaining the basis of her assessment of the project.

External locus of evaluation—The boy's Social Studies book is handed back with many crosses in the margins, and corrections of grammar and spelling written all over the pages. At the foot of the last page, the teacher has written "Poor! Is this the best you can manage in 6 weeks?" A mark of $2/10$ figures prominently. The teacher hands the book to the boy in silence and glares at him for a few seconds while he shuffles his feet and hangs his head.

"What do you think I thought when I read that?" she asks in a disgusted tone. "It's dirty and untidy—a real mess. How much time did you put into this masterpiece? Half an hour?" She turns to a drawing of the wheat-producing regions marked on a map. "Look at that! Couldn't you even copy it correctly from your book? And what, may I ask is this word *wheet*? Couldn't you get even that right? You knew very well what I wanted. I put out some of last year's best projects for you to copy from if you had to. This is terrible. Take it away and don't bring it back until it's done properly." The boy goes off muttering with resentment.

Guided self-evaluation—The assignment has a number of questions and question marks in various places, and some words and phrases are lightly underlined. No mark is showing, and no final, definitive judgment has been written in at the end. The boy approaches in hangdog manner. "Well, David, what do you think of your project?" the teacher asks. He mumbles unintelligibly (he knows that it is a poor job). "Is there anything you could have improved?" Silence. "What about these?" She points to finger marks on the first page. "They're smudges," David mumbles. "I could rub them off." "All right, let's do that," she says, and there is a pause while some repairs are carried out with the eraser.

"Now let's have a look at this map," continues the teacher. "Here's the page in the book. Can you see any way to make your map easier for you to understand when you are thinking about the places where they grow wheat?" "It's kind of crooked in that corner," volunteers David. She seizes the opportunity. "Do you think you could make it more helpful now?" she asks, and he agrees that he could improve it.

They continue in this way for a while; then the teacher asks, "Do you reckon you could have learned more about wheat while you were doing the project?" He agrees that he could have. "If your very best work got $^{10}/_{10}$, what would you give this project?" He says perhaps $^{5}/_{10}$. She then asks him how he would go about making it more like his very best work, and he says that he would have got some books from the library that told about wheat. She asks him if he would like to have another go at the project, and he says that he would. They arrange that he will find out some things about wheat and find some illustrations, and that he will bring them back to her to talk about making them into a project. David then departs, to produce a good piece of work, it is to be hoped.

The emphasis has continually been on satisfaction of personal standards. However, the teacher has not accepted anything that the student cared to give her, through fear that any evaluative process would stunt creativity. The student already knew that he had not really made much of an effort, and the teacher's acceptance of this would only have confirmed his belief that any old thing from him is good enough. However, the teacher has drawn his attention to the worst defects and has planted ways of setting about remedying them in his mind (she has "guided" the evaluation). At the same time, she has referred back to internal standards, such as a sense of achievement, and to the idea that the project is meant to be useful to him personally rather than to meet some external authority's demands (she has stressed "self-evaluation"). In this way, she has utilized guided self-evaluation.

The patterns of encouragement and discouragement, rewards and punishments, can be summarized by saying that the teacher should:

- offer recognition and approval of creative achievements,
- give students opportunities to communicate their ideas,
- treat unusual questions and ideas with interest,

- stress the value of novel ideas in solving problems,
- provide opportunities for students to play with ideas,
- encourage delay of judgment,
- provide opportunities for nonevaluated classroom activities, and
- place great emphasis on genuine self-evaluation.

Failing to sponsor a creative child—Typical of most elementary schools are talent days. The school I attended was no different. One day, when I was 9 years old, the big day arrived. When it was my turn to perform before the class, I was most excited. I marched to the front of the classroom, stood in front of the piano, and announced the piece I was about to play and the composer, who was myself: "Nothingness," by Margaret Bailey. This was followed by thunderous laughter and questioning about the name of the piece. Perhaps it was that I was naive, but I did not feel or think they were questioning me as to whether I had composed this miniature masterpiece. My pride was a little out of joint, but my enthusiasm to continue and play held firm. I was convinced that their laughter would change to awe. The piece I was to play was not comparable to a one-handed, one-octave "Mary Had a Little Lamb." My predictions were correct. They were awed but also skeptical. The laughter and snickers I had previously received were painful but did not compare with the humiliation and defeat I felt when the teacher (in front of the whole class) questioned me as to whether I was taking credit for my own work or someone else's. Her questioning took the form of outright disbelief—she made a statement perfectly clearly in the grammatical form of a question. My response to this was tearful and resentful. I continued to perform in talent days, but I made sure that nobody knew that I had composed any of my pieces. It was 10 years later before I had the self-confidence to give myself credit where it was due (with regard to music).

The teacher failed this student very badly. How? What should she have done? Before reading further, answer this question taking into account the concept of *guided self-evaluation.*

Alienating and isolating the creative child—This happened when I was in grade 6. As the year progressed, I was beginning to give my teacher the benefit of the doubt. This later appeared to be premature. I received no insults about my artistic talent, but I fell subject to the label of class deviant. This needs considerable explanation, but was due primarily to my fear of failing and my fear of humiliation, brought about by a terrible lisp and occasional stuttering. Consequently, I kept my mouth shut in class—even when I was questioned or requested to read before the class.

What my teacher then did was not to my liking. She started a routine which I was to become familiar with. "You are capable of doing much better work than you're producing." Rather than helping me along with the academic curriculum, she literally had me leave the classroom to paint, draw, and sketch. This suited my fancy. I was talented at drawing, and she recognized it. However, due to this I fell behind in academic and (somewhat) social skills. I was alienated from the rest of the class—labelled the teacher's pet due to all this attention, and also labelled the class moron, because somewhere along the line I had missed mastering the skills of mathematical division.

I found myself in a bind. If I asked to come into the class in the morning, I was told I had this exceptional talent that she wished to foster. But when I fell short of her academic expectations, I found myself subject to being accused of laziness and defiance. As far as I could see, I couldn't win, so I continued down the merry path of alienation, submissiveness, and outright hostility. I managed to pass with average marks that year, a developed artistic talent, and plenty of confusion as to what I was, who I was, and what I was supposed to do or be.

The teacher recognized this girl's creative talent. However, her efforts at fostering it had unpleasant effects for the student. Where did the teacher go wrong?

Taking the creative student under one's wing—When I was 16 I found Literature class stimulating, but somehow I only performed well in written work. Because my written work was so much better than my verbal classroom performance, the teacher often queried whether I had really done the written work myself.

One particular assignment I recall vividly was a short story. I was delighted. The subject was open, and I could let my imagination run wild. I proudly handed in this assignment, confident that I would do well. My teacher said that the story was "magnificent." I should have known better, but I was so pleased I failed to recognize his disbelief. He soon brought this to my attention. This resulted in a verbal battle. I pleaded that it was my own work and my own idea. The miserable wretch promptly marched me to the principal's office. Praise to the principal! He had more confidence in my abilities than my Literature teacher. He, quite wisely I thought, transferred me into his own class. He encouraged me to come up with my own ideas and praised me when I did well, although he criticized my failures. My marks went sky high, and by the end of the year I was not so reluctant to speak up in class. I stand firmly by the opinion that he did more for my personal and emotional growth than any other teacher I have ever had the misfortune of contending with.

What special needs of this creative student did the principal attend to? What characteristic problems of creative children did he help her to deal with?

Accepting and encouraging divergent ideas—A grade 1 class is learning to print. The teacher has been asking various children to come out to the front of the class and make various letters on the blackboard. This is meant to be a reward, and the teacher has been encouraging and supportive with shy or nervous children, creating opportunities for them to achieve public success. The teacher asks: "Who would like to come out to the board and draw on it for me a .... " She pauses dramatically while the children wait eagerly to see which letter she will nominate. "A *d*!" Many hands shoot up, amid cries of "Miss! Miss!" The teacher chooses one little girl. This particular child is often reticent and reluctant to answer, although she does her work well enough. The teacher has also noticed that the girl has poor social relations with her classmates and is sometimes the butt of their teasing. The child runs out to the blackboard and grabs the chalk with obvious enthusiasm. She makes an initial stroke on the board but then hesitates and stops. She stands at the board in indecision for a few moments, then turns to the teacher. "Please, Miss Henderson, the *d* is the one with the big belly sticking out, but I can't remember which way his tummy pokes." The other children start to snigger and jeer.

What should the teacher do? The child had developed her own mnemonic to help her remember the shape of the letter *d*. If you think about it, it is something like a stick figure with a pot belly. (My own mnemonic as a child was to remember that a *b* consisted of a bat and a ball.) The "big belly" is even better, as it applies to the capital letter as well as the small letter. Although not what one would immediately expect, the remark about the letter's "tummy" makes sense and even shows a certain ingenuity, along with a fresh conceptualization of the nature of the letters of the alphabet. Why is the way in which the teacher handled this situation important, as far as fostering creativity is concerned? How could the teacher use this incident as the jumping-off point for an interaction with her pupils of a kind likely to foster creative thinking? What potential blocking factors are looming as a trap for the teacher?

Destroying peer relations—In a senior physics class, the teacher has been solving on the blackboard a problem in mechanics. He reaches a point at which the numbers have obviously become absurd, and stops in some confusion. He stands back from the board and tries to locate the error that he knows he must have made. Embarrassingly, he cannot find it immediately. At this point, one student puts up his hand, then explains that the error involves the mixing of force and mass. The teacher agrees that this is the problem, thanks the student, and makes the necessary correction. He then uses the opportunity for some class revision of the point on which he had erred, by asking the student to explain the difference between force and mass. This is done correctly, and some valuable revision takes place.

The teacher then addresses the class in general: "I don't know what I had to wait so long for someone to have the brains to point out what I did wrong. Still, what can you expect from people who are asleep half the time and in a daze for the rest of it?" Not content with that, he turns to the student who found the error. "Thank heaven someone in the class had his wits about him!

Thank you very much, Keith, for helping me out. It's pity that these other clots couldn't have done as well! At this point, Keith wishes that the floor would open up and swallow him. His classmates glare at him. Finally, however, one student asks the teacher if he would clarify part of the explanation just given. The teacher replies: "I don't see any need for that. As far as I am concerned, Keith here has made it all perfectly clear. I'm certainly not going to ask him to go over the whole thing again just for you!" The lesson then continued in subdued silence.

Suppose that Keith is well known as an answerer of questions, often in terms that most classmates cannot understand. How could the teacher have responded in this particular situation in order to increase both Keith's and other students' willingness to make suggestions or offer explanations? What aspects of the teacher's response in the situation described was commendable? What aspects of his behavior were of a blocking nature? What sort of effect on Keith's relations with other students would this incident be likely to have, especially if it were repeated in different forms in a number of classes? How might the kind of teacher response described here affect Keith's self-image? How should the teacher have handled the whole exchange? What pitfalls need to be watched out for in this kind of situation, if creativity is to be fostered?

FURTHER READING

de Bono, E. (1971). *The uses of lateral thinking*. Harmondsworth, UK: Penguin.

Hudson, L. (1966). *Contrary imaginations*. London: Methuen.

Pickard, E. M. (1979). *The development of creative ability*. London: National Foundation for Educational Research.

Torrance, E. P. (1963). *Fostering creativity in the classroom*. Minneapolis: University of Minnesota Press.

Torrance, E. P. (1983). *Creativity in the classroom*. Washington, DC: National Educational Association.

7

Training Creativity

SPECIAL PROGRAMS

A number of procedures for "training" creativity have been developed in the last 200 years, including both short-term and long-term programs. The variety of procedures which exist is illustrated by the fact that Treffinger and Gowan (1971) were able to describe nearly 50 different approaches (also see reviews by Mansfield, Busse, & Krepelka, 1978).

Short-term Procedures

Davis and Scott (1971) listed more than 20 creativity-facilitating activities, including "attribute listing," "idea matrix," "synectic thinking," "creativity toolbox," and "morphological analysis." Endriss (1982) developed a range of brief "games" such as "bridge building," "idea production," "transformations," and "creative connections." All of these are aimed at raising people's level of creativity with the help of simple training procedures requiring only a small amount of time. The idea behind them is that people acquire techniques for getting ideas or going directly to the unusual, that they develop interest in and motivation for thinking of this kind, or that blocking factors such as fear of letting oneself go or lack of trust in one's own ideas are eliminated. Hudson (1968) reported that simply giving students 10 examples of unusual responses (in this case, unusual cases for an elastic band) greatly increased their scores on a divergent thinking test. Maltzman, Simon, Raskin, and Licht (1960) reported a simple cognitive procedure in which people were required to think up unusual associations to stimulus words. This was said to lead to lasting increases in originality after only a few minutes training. More recent studies have attempted to improve scores on creativity test by means of a number of other training procedures. Belcher (1975) showed children a film in which an actor worked on a creativity test; Dansky (1980) allowed children to play with materials similar to those found in tests; and Ziv (1976) played a tape of a famous comedian to children, in order to increase their willingness to use humor. Glover and Gary (1976) employed the principles of learning and attempted to increase the frequency of divergent responses by the application of appropriate reinforcements.

Despite frequently reported success in the raising of test scores, there is only limited evidence that training actually increases creativity. Rather, it seems to improve performance only on activities which closely resemble the training procedure. In a detailed review of the evidence, Rump (1979) came to the conclusion that the effects of training are at their strongest when the criterion closely resembles the training procedure, and at their weakest when this similarity is low. In the case of personality, interests, and preferences, only limited effects are obtained. Consequently, it is possible to conclude that short-term training procedures have little effect on general creative skills, attitudes, values, self-image, and motivation. There is even a danger that creativity-training procedures have the opposite effect from the desired one. For example, children can become aware in the course of training that certain kinds of behavior are preferred by the teacher and can alter their behavior accordingly. Although children may be encouraged by the training to work hard on the various tasks which they are presented, they can learn that it is easy to give "original" answers if one engages in hair splitting, gives rambling answers without regard to accuracy or relevance, or offers banalities in the name of creativity. In this way, "creativity" can quickly degenerate to a special form of conformity. Commenting on brainstorming, Parloff and Handlon (1964) suggested that, instead of becoming more creative as a result of offering ideas freely, people may simply become less self-critical.

More Comprehensive Programs

Mansfield et al. (1978) have reviewed five relevant creativity-training programs: the Productive Thinking Program, the Purdue Creative Thinking Program, the Osborn/Parnes Program, the Myers-Torrance Workbooks, and the Khatena Training Method. An overview of the special characteristics of these programs is presented in Table 7.1.

According to Mansfield et al. (1978), the Parnes program and the Khatena Training Method have the most convincing records. A characteristic shared by both of these is their breadth of training. Additionally, the training is not linked to a fixed set of materials. Mansfield et al. expressed the belief that brainstorming, which is emphasized by the Parnes program, has been an effective element. The better evaluative studies of the Productive Thinking Program are said to have provided only "modest

Table 7.1.   Main characteristics of several creativity programs.*

Program	Age Level	Material	Aimed at Promoting
Productive Thinking Program	Fifth- and Sixth-grade pupils	Booklets containing cartoons	i) problem-solving abilities ii) attitudes toward problem solving
Purdue Creative Thinking	Fourth grade pupils	Audiotapes and accompanying printed exercises	Verbal and figural fluency, flexibility, originality, & elaboration
Parnes Program	High school & college students	No special materials	Getting many ideas Primary emphasis on brainstorming, with separation of idea generation and idea evaluation
Myers-Torrance Workbooks	Elementary school pupils	Workbooks containing exercises	Perceptual cognitive abilities needed for creativity
Khatena Training Method	Adults and children	No special materials. Simple teacher-made aids are employed	i) ability to break away from the obvious ii) transposing ideas iii) seeing analogies iv) restructuring information v) synthesis of ideas

*This table is reprinted with permission from Mcleod and Cropley, *Fostering academic excellence,* Copyright 1989, Pergamon Press PLC.

evidence of the program's effectiveness" (p. 530). The verdict on the Purdue Creative Thinking Program is similarly pessimistic: "The...soundest (study) provided the least evidence for the program's effectiveness" (p. 551). Of the Myers—Torrance Workbooks, Mansfield et al. consider that "the paucity of soundly designed research is surprising, considering their popularity...There is no evidence that the workbooks improve performance on measures substantially different from those used in the exercises" (p. 531). In other words, it is not at all clear that the effects of creativity training will be reflected in real-life creative accomplishments.

Torrance (1972) himself acknowledged that many researchers would be likely to discredit his evaluation of some 142 studies of attempts to enhance creativity. However, he maintained that many procedures really do have a positive effect, especially those which emphasize, not only cognitive (getting ideas, combining information, and so on) but also affective aspects (having the courage to try something different, wanting to reach a novel solution, and the like). Franklin and Richards (1977) demonstrated that deliberate attempts to increase divergent thinking (i.e., formal training) are more effective than simply reducing the level of formality, or exposing children to a wider variety of experiences. However, Cropley and Feuring (1971) showed that the results of such training are not necessarily equally effective with girls and boys, and that the effects of training depended strongly on the conditions under which the criterion data were obtained. Thus, it is apparent that there is a need to exercise a certain level of general reservation about the effectiveness of programs designed to foster creativity, even though they represent at least a step in the right direction and can be an enjoyable experience in their own right.

As Wallach (1985) put it, the basic idea of promoting creativity by means of appropriate training procedures is by no means foolish. Unfortunately, simply training divergent thinking does not seem to achieve the desired results. To adapt an analogy suggested by Wallach, teaching sprinters preparing for a race how to hammer down the starting blocks is not irrelevant to their chances of running a fast time, but it can hardly be regarded as training them to run faster. To take an actual example he mentioned: Students in a creative-writing program practiced with divergent-thinking tests for 2 years, and at the end they were noticeably better on such tests—but their writing had hardly become more creative at all! In order to foster creativity, it is necessary to develop procedures which relate directly to the area of achievement, in which performance is to be improved and which involve the kinds of activity which are to be carried out better. Thus, creativity-fostering activities that can be applied to school work and that relate to the things students do in class are needed. What this means for creativity-fostering instruction in the classroom will be outlined in the following section.

SOME WELL-KNOWN TECHNIQUES

Although the procedures depicted in following sections were developed at different times and for purposes other than education (for instance, in management training or in industrial settings), they all have a number of common elements, including:

1. Formation of analogies,
2. Building up of chains of ideas or associations,
3. Redefinition of the question or problem, and
4. Looking at existing information in new ways.

These elements are achieved, among other things, by breaking free of strictly logical, linear thinking in favor of "divergent" or "lateral" thinking, by opening one's mind to material from the unconscious, or by allowing ideas to "flow," "well up," or "stream." Among the conditions which facilitate the emergence of creative thinking in the sense just outlined are:

1. A relaxed atmosphere,
2. Possession of knowledge about creativity and its facilitation,
3. Working in a group of people who are similarly skilled, and
4. Working with an appropriately trained group leader.

Creative Problem Solving

An activity which requires productive thinking, and at the same time offers good opportunities for promoting it, is problem solving. It is apparent that the modern world is beset with problems of major dimensions, such as how to achieve world peace, eliminate disease, and feed the ever-growing world population. Although these present a fascinating challenge for clever and creative children, they can quickly assume such vast dimensions that they become mere exercises in unverifiable, unchecked, unevaluated fantasy. In keeping with Renzulli's (1982) suggestion that we should concentrate on "real" programs—not that war, disease, and hunger are not genuine problems, but they offer little prospect for actual application of children's ideas—it is possible to identify problems of more modest dimensions which still present a challenge and provide an opportunity for exercising the same mental processes as the vast problems just listed. The possibility of dealing with "little" problems has helped make creative problem solving a popular instructional activity for fostering creativity.

Feldhusen and Treffinger (1980, p. 33) identified three phases in the problem-solving process:

1. awareness, a motivating factor;
2. problem formulation, when the problem is defined and ideas arise for plausible solution strategies; and
3. searching, during which information is gathered to be associated with the formulation of viable hypotheses.

These phases have to be operationalized and have generally been broken down into a series of steps for the purpose of creative problem solving (Torrance, Torrance, Williams, & Horng, 1978, p. 5), along the following lines:

1. encounter a problem "situation";
2. brainstorm possible specific problems stemming from the situation that has been presented;

3. operationalized the problem to be attacked, stating it clearly, in an "attackable" form;
4. brainstorm alternative solutions;
5. brainstorm criteria against which to judge alternative solutions;
6. rank available solutions according to the criteria that have been adopted; and
7. select and improve the best solution, and present ("sell") it for judging or adoption.

In addition to the procedures just outlined, it is possible to list tactics for finding new perspectives on problems, thus "breaking" them open. A number of these are stated here as suggestions:

Reverse the Problem. It is frequently possible to obtain valuable insights into solving a problem by reversing the way in which it is examined. An example of this kind of problem solving taken from mythology is the way in which the innkeeper, Procrustes, made his bed fit all guests. If the bed proved to be too small for a very large client or too large for a very small one, then the guests were the wrong size, not the bed. Consequently, where the guest was too big for the bed Procrustes simply cut off the parts of the guest which projected beyond the end of the bed! Similarly, where clients were too small for the bed (not the bed too big for the client), Procrustes simply had them stretched on a rack until they fitted. Although this kind of behavior is not being advanced as laudable, it provides an example of how reversing the problem can lead to a solution.

Consider the End Result. Another technique for developing creative ideas is somewhat similar to that of reversing the problem. In this case, attention is focused on the desired end result, and the problem is though of from that point of view.

The story of a young lady who avoided an unwanted suitor in this way is a good illustration of the point. She was required to choose out of a bag one of two pebbles which had been picked up by the suitor from the path on which they were standing. Because her father was deeply in debt to the man, she had to accept his suggestion that he would place a black and a white pebble inside a bag and that she would pick one. If she chose the white, her father's debts would be forgiven and she would go free. If she chose the black, her father's debts would be forgiven, but she would have to marry the man. In fact the man cheated by bending down and selecting two black pebbles, which he smuggled into the bag. Fortunately the girl saw that he had done this. However, her problem was that if she simply exposed the trick, her father would not be released from the debt he owed. If she chose a pebble, it seemed that she would be doomed to marry the man she hated.

She solved the problem by thinking about the end result. What was required was not so much that she choose a white pebble, but that a black pebble remained in the bag. The problem of choosing a white pebble was impossible, because there were no white pebbles in the bag. However, the problem of leaving a black pebble was absurdly simple, because there were nothing but black pebbles in the bag! She chose a pebble but, without allowing anybody to see it, dropped it to the gravel path on which they were standing, and kicked it away among the other stones, where it was immediately lost. She then apologized for dropping the pebble, but pointed out that it would be very easy to find out what color it had been by examining the color of the pebble remaining in the bag. Of course, that pebble was black, and the suitor, who did not wish to be exposed as a cheat, was forced to admit that she must have chosen a white one.

Focus on the Dominant Idea. In a problem-solving situation, the real problem is sometimes submerged or lost sight of, and it is often very valuable to pick out what it is that is actually required and express it as simply as possible in order to strip away all irrelevant details. Focusing on the heart of the problem in this way frequently leads to extremely simple but effective solutions.

During the Berlin airlift, shortly after the Second World War, aircraft carrying food and other essentials to the people of Berlin were landing at intervals of only a few minutes. A serious problem which threatened to end the whole airlift arose when winter ice and fog made visibility and landing conditions extremely poor. If a plane did not make a perfect approach on the first attempt, it was certain to cause a crash when it attempted to circle the airport and make a new landing run, because the next aircraft was only a minute or so behind it. The only safe procedure was to interrupt the flow of arriving aircraft to provide time for a second landing attempt. As a result the point was actually reached when many takeoffs had to be cancelled, because conditions had grown so bad that planes were repeatedly missing their landing approaches and then blocking the airspace with their second attempts. However, this meant that the airlift was not working, because food was not getting through in sufficient quantities.

The problem appeared to be insoluble at first, for there was no way in which a plane that had not made a good approach could climb, circle the airport, make a new approach, and land successfully in the seconds that were allowed before the following aircraft arrived at the scene. However, analysis of the key idea quickly revealed a simple solution. The real problem when a plane missed a landing was not how to get it back into a position from which it could land within seconds, but how to clear it out of the airport's immediate vicinity in a very short time. The first problem— that of achieving a second approach and landing in a few seconds—was impossible. The second and real problem was simple. All that was required was that a plane which missed its landing continue flying straight on out of the airport's air space and return to its base. Its load of supplies was not delivered, but the following flights were not disrupted.

Discard Irrelevant Constraints. In a somewhat similar way, good ideas are often blocked by self-imposed constraints that are not inherent in a situation but are assumed by the person who is doing the thinking. The story of Columbus and the egg is an example. At a dinner, the host is supposed to have challenged anyone present to make an egg stand on its end. Many of the guests tried to balance the egg either on the smaller or the larger end, without success. Finally, Columbus took the egg, tapped it gently on the table, but with sufficient force to crack the shell and form a flat spot, and then stood it up without difficulty. Amid a hail of protests that this was not fair, Columbus pointed out that no one had at any time said that the egg was not to be broken. Because of their social conditioning to avoid breaking eggs, the people who had tried and failed had imposed unnecessary restrictions on themselves.

Use Fantasy. Acceptance of the idea that thinking is a serious business and play is a waste of time may lead children to avoid fantasy. Although it is very important that children understand the difference between fantasy and reality, it is well known that many fantastic ideas, such as those of Jules Verne, have since become reality. Consequently, children who consciously and deliberately utilize fantasy as a way of obtaining divergent ideas may frequently find their creative thinking facilitated. This is particularly true when ideas originating in fantasy are subsequently subjected to guided self-evaluation, in order to tease out their practically useful elements.

Future Problem Solving

Future problem solving (FPS) was initiated by Torrance in the U.S. in 1974 and rapidly gained popularity, being perceived by participating teachers and students as enjoyable and beneficial (Torrance et al., 1978). Future problem solving represents a special form of creative problem solving in which the possibility of any external validation is eliminated by the very nature of the exercise—topics for the programs between 1982 and 1984 included UFOs, ocean communities, nuclear disarmament, and genetic engineering (Hoomes, 1984). However, Torrance (1978, p. 15) advised, "if always dealing with future situations bothers them, occasionally bring out a current situation. The newspaper is chock full of ideas." The posing of the problem to be attacked is generally of the form "How might we...?" or "In what ways might we...?" (Torrance et al., 1978, p. 14). Students study the topic mainly through reading books, newspapers, and magazines, supplemented by television and talks with available experts. In view of the global, strategic, geopolitical nature of many of the problems tackled, students ought to have direct access to the perspectives of countries other than their own. Shortwave radio, foreign newspapers, and overseas TV via satellite provide excellent means of becoming acquainted with a total spectrum of current political perspectives of many future problems.

Brainstorming

Brainstorming is a technique which can be used at every stage of creative problem solving. Indeed, as Feldhusen and Treffinger (1980, p. 98) noted, it "can conveniently be used in nearly every subject area and situation." Perhaps one of the most spectacular examples of the success of brainstorming by extremely gifted people occurred in World War II at Bletchley Park, England, where mathematicians, scholars, crossword puzzle wizards, and creative writers such as Ian Fleming, the creator of James Bond, were assembled. Their accomplishments included a contribution to the breaking of the German Enigma code.

Brainstorming is a group activity in which each member of the group is encouraged to put forward ideas, so that, as the session develops, ideas flow "fast and heavy" (Basadur et al., 1990; Osborn, 1953). In order for brainstorming to catch fire, participants must not feel inhibited, and so criticism of any idea—no matter how implausible or wild—is suspended during the production stage of the proceedings. Torrance et al. (1978) listed four basic rules:

1. Criticism is ruled out.
2. Freewheeling is welcomed: the wilder the ideas the better.
3. Quantity is wanted, because the greater the number of ideas produced, the greater the probability that original, useful ideas will emerge.
4. Combination and improvement are sought: Group members are encouraged to "hitch-hike" on the ideas of others.

A variety of scenarios is possible for conducting a brainstorming session. If, as some suggest, members of the group are seated in a circle and encouraged to call out their ideas, the session may be dominated by more extroverted individuals, and potentially valuable contributions from students who are more reticent may be lost. One procedure which has been found to be practical with groups from grade 4 to senior university administrators is summarized in point form in Table 7.2. Preferably, the group should consist of between 10 and 12 individuals; larger groups should be divided into subgroups, the results from which are pooled and distributed later by the overall coordinator.

Table 7.2.   Steps in brainstorming*

1. The group appoints two scribes/recorders:
   (1) one writes suggestions on the blackboard (plenty of blackboard space is needed) or on large sheets of paper that can be displayed around the room. Each suggestion is numbered.
   (2) the other writes the suggestions on paper, for later identification of items.

2. For approximately 10 minutes, each person writes his or her suggestions on individual sheets of paper. No talking or discussion occurs during this period.

3. A round robin then takes place during which group members, in turn, read out their most important suggestion, and the scribes record. No comment or discussion of suggestions yet, but hitchhiking is permitted; i.e., members of the group may add to an existing suggestion if their own suggestion represents an extension of one already on the board.

4. Step 3 is repeated. Normally, this procedure will continue until everyone has literally dried up. If time is limited, it might be necessary to limit the procedure to four or five rounds.

5. Group discussion takes place concerning equivalence of suggestions and the merging of different suggestions. Scribes erase, transfer, and amend as required.

6. Each member of the group ranks what he or she considers to be the most important 10 suggestions on the board, in order of perceived importance. The suggestions are identified by number; i.e., there is no need to writer the suggestions in full, as scribe No. 2 has recorded the suggestion numbers.

7. Depending on the time available, the results may be analyzed on the spot, but it will generally be more convenient for each member of the group to hand in the ranked suggestions to a scribe who passes them on to the workshop leader.

8. The conclusions are made available later, after analysis.

*Reprinted with permission from McLeod & Cropley, *Fostering academic excellence,* Copyright 1989, Pergamon Press PLC.

There are various ways to treat the rankings. The simplest is simply to tally how many times a suggestion is included in the list of each group member, and the suggestion which is included the most times is the "winner." Alternatively, the median ranking of each suggestion is determined (with a rank of 11 being awarded to a suggestion each time it is not included in the top 10 for any group member). A useful exercise for computer-oriented students (and a potential point of departure for a study and discussion of different voting procedures) would be to analyze the rankings according to a "distributed preferences" procedure, such as is used in Australian elections.

Synectics

Synectics is a procedure for bringing together elements which do not seem to belong together (Gordon, 1961). Two major principles of synectics are "making the strange familiar" and "making the familiar strange." The idea is that unusual, apparently irrelevant or little-known objects or processes are seen in a new light by emphasizing elements which fit in well with the problem at hand, although they would not normally be regarded as relevant (making the strange familiar), or that well-known objects or processes are looked at as though one does not really know what they are for, although the facts about them are known (making the familiar strange). As in brainstorming, synectics is usually conducted in a group (although the two basic principles can also be carried out by an individual person working alone).

Group members are confronted with some problem to be solved. Initially, members of the group simply suggest objects or processes which actually have some relationship to the requirements of the problem solution, although they would not normally be regarded as related to it— for instance, a member of a group trying to develop a form of paint which would never fade mentioned that some algae never lose their color, thus "making the strange familiar" by redefining something (algae) which normally has nothing to do with the problem in question (paint) in terms of the familiar. Subsequently, a paint that forms a coat or layer adhering to the surface of the painted object (instead of soaking into it) was developed. Similarly, to invent an example, it would be possible to redefine a window (something with which we are all familiar) as a device for permitting communication through soundproof barriers, thus making the familiar strange.

A synectic thinking session could have the following steps:

1. group leader describes the problem which is to be solved;
2. group members spontaneously offer key words which reduce the problem to its basic elements;
3. the group leader tries to find abstract definitions of the problem, using only two of these key words (i.e., to make the familiar strange);
4. participants suggest analogies to be found in everyday life, in nature, in industry, or technology, and so on (i.e., they attempt to make the strange familiar); and
5. participants imagine that they are a living example of the analogy mentioned in the previous step, and picture how they would feel in the situation in question.

This approach is in some ways related to brainstorming. However, it is particularly interesting in that it seeks to systematize the process of seeing connections between elements of experience and knowledge that are not normally regarded as belonging together. In this respect, it constitutes a procedure for promoting purposeful, goal-directed divergent thinking.

The 635 Method

Six problem solvers, working individually, each write down three suggestions for the problem in question without evaluating them, in a maximum
of 5 minutes. Each person then passes on his or her own sheet of paper to
the next person on, say, the left, receiving the sheet of the right-hand
neighbor in return. Participants then spend 5 minutes elaborating their
neighbors' suggestions or formulating new suggestions which have been
prompted by those of the neighbors, subsequently passing on the paper to
the left once more and receiving a paper from the right. This is repeated
until all sheets of paper have been seen by all six participants. Subsequently, the group examines the six sheets and evaluates the solutions
proffered. This approach avoids some problems which arise when suggestions for solutions have to be made orally and under direct observation of
the other members of the group. It also offers a written record of the
emergence of the ideas developed and of the contributions of individual
participants, recognizable by means of their handwriting.

CASE STUDIES

Imposing unnecessary restraints—It happened in grade 3. The teacher asked
me to tell her which of the numbers between 1 and 10 could be divided by 2.
We had been learning about odd and even numbers; of course, what she
wanted was for me to say that the even numbers could be divided by 2—2, 4,
6, and 8. I really bugged her when I said that they could all be divided by 2.
She told me to try again, as though she thought I hadn't understood the
question or something. But I gritted my teeth and told her again that they
could all be divided by 2. So then she said something about; "All right, what
about 5? How can you divide 5 by 2?" The answer was easy, of course. Five
divided by two is $2\frac{1}{2}$! She had got it into her head that we weren't supposed
to know anything about fractions, which I did know about. If you didn't cut
back your ideas so that they fitted the limits she had in her mind, you were
wrong. She taught me to find out what the hidden limits were, and to keep my
ideas inside those limits, even if I knew that they weren't the real limits. Five
divided by 2 *is* $2\frac{1}{2}$!

Problems are often made more difficult because people impose unnecessary restrictions. This closes thinking rather than opening it.

Focusing on the key point—I was an enthusiastic math student. As a matter
of fact, I'm now a mathematics teacher, so that my own teachers must have
got me started somehow. One problem I remember really got me interested—
I was the only one who got it right, and I reckon that might have started me
off. Our teacher was revising fractions with us when he gave us the old

problem about something which doubles its size every day. The one he gave us went like this: "Some lichen is growing on a rock. Every day it doubles its area. The rock was finally covered after exactly 20 days. After how many days was it exactly half-covered?" We were all racking our brains trying to get the answer when he said quietly, "Remember that its size one day is half what it will be the next day." That was the key for me. I saw that you had to concentrate on the fact that covering the whole rock was double covering half of it, so that it must have doubled from half the rock to the whole rock in one day. The correct answer was 19 days, of course. When time was up, I was the only one who had finished. The others were all writing down things like "X + 2X + 4X" and so on, and asking how big the rock was and that sort of thing. The teacher made me realize that the real point may sometimes be hidden and yet in full view.

This principle can be applied in other subjects apart from math. The important thing is the manner in which the teacher gave the hint. Before reading further, consider how this was connected with creativity.

Using fantasy and play—When I was in grade 3, we had a story about a frog who got all dressed up in his best clothes and then got swallowed by a duck or some other bird like that. Perhaps it was an owl. Anyway, the teacher read us the story which was really a poem, now that I think about it a bit. I felt very sorry for the poor old froggy. Then the teacher asked us to think how the frog could get out of the bird's belly and save itself. She told us to imagine that we were really there in the bird's stomach. What would it be like? All cold and wet and squishy. What could a frog do to try to get out?

I'm not sure whether or not we succeeded in getting the frog out, but she taught me a good lesson. You can actually let your imagination go and solve many problem by having the fantasy that you are living the experience. It doesn't have to be something alive; you can imagine you are a lump of rock, or a number in an equation, or a note in a song, and work out what it really feels like. Suppose that a number in a sum really wants to get solved correctly. Imagine what it feels like—where does it want to go, what does it want to be? I get lots of good ideas like that.

It is very possible to "think yourself inside problems" through the use of fantasy, but this is probably one of the least employed of people's thinking capacities. Why?

Using a familiar object is an uncommon way—A high school class in Science has been learning about barometers. The teacher has mentioned other uses of the barometer in addition to its role in weather forecasting. In order to excite the students' interest, he has discussed the use of barometers as altimeters in aeroplanes, pointing out that a barometer can be used to estimate altitude, for pressure drops with increasing altitude. There is some discussion of the necessity to adjust the zero position according to the distance above sea level of the initial ground level. The teacher then decides to see if the children have actually grasped the principle of barometric function that permits its use as an altimeter. He asks them to indicate how a barometer could be used to ascertain the height of a building. Eventually, one boy puts up his hand, and the teacher asks him to explain how he would do it.

The boy replies: "You could take it to the top of the building. When you got there, you could drop it off the roof and start counting in seconds. You would have to watch the barometer falling through the air, and keep on counting all the time. When you saw it hit the ground, you would stop counting. Now you can calculate the height of the building from the formula $s = 1/2\ at^2$."

What idea-getting principle is exemplified by this solution? Although not a very practical solution, this one would work. Consequently, how could you get the particular student to reject it as a practical procedure, without simply telling him that it was wrong and without implying that the idea was absurd or crazy? How could this episode be used to initiate a review of some of the laws of elementary mechanics?

Beginning from the end—A class at the middle secondary school level is having a geometry lesson. They have been given some problems to solve in which they are required to prove that certain pairs of triangles are congruent. One problem has proven to be particularly difficult. However, one girl has "seen" an intermediate step that makes it possible to show that two angles are equal, and thus provides the last of the three conditions needed to establish congruence. Subsequently, when asked to explain how she had worked out that the two angles were equal, she explains: "I started off by assuming that the triangles really were congruent. Then I went over in my mind all of the things that could be proved by someone who knew that they were congruent. I asked myself how you could prove the things that had actually been given as already true. I turned it back to front and used what we had to show to prove that what we had been given was really true. Then I saw that you could prove the givens if the triangles were congruent, so I knew how to prove they were congruent, using the given facts instead of proving them. I just turned it around and started at the end!

Although the girl's explanation is a little hard to follow, what idea getting technique had she employed? What is the connection between this kind of thinking and creativity? How would you proceed from this point if this happened in your classroom? Consider various teacher reactions from the point of view of blocking or fostering creativity.

FURTHER READING

Adams, J.L. (1980). *Conceptual blockbusting—A guide to better ideas.* New York: Norton.

Davis, G.A., & Scott, J.A. (1971). *Training creative thinking.* New York: Holt, Rinehart and Winston.

Lett, W.R. (Ed.). (1976). *Creativity and education.* Melbourne: Australian International Press and Publication.

Stein, M.I. (1974). *Stimulating creativity* (Vol. 1). New York: Academic Press.

Stein, M.I. (1974). *Stimulating creativity* (Vol. 2). New York: Academic Press.

Torrance, E.P. (1965). *Rewarding creative behavior.* Englewood Cliffs, NJ: Prentice-Hall.

8

Classroom Activities

GENERAL TACTICS

As Williams (1976a) put it, what is needed in the classroom is a "responsive environment" (p. 18) or a "safe psychological base." This promotes fluent, flexible, original, and elaborative thinking (Williams, 1976b). The flow of ideas must be "unfrozen" (Hare, 1982, p. 158); this includes, not only thinking skills, but also the "courage to create" (Motamedi, 1982, p. 84). Children need help: to resist the temptation to accept the first, plausible answer to a problem; to see ideas in broader contexts; to visualize possibilities; to use imagination (Torrance & Hall, 1980). Such thinking activities are facilitated, not only by appropriate knowledge and skills, but also by personal properties such as self-confidence, curiosity, openness to experience, or willingness to be provoked and excited by new possibilities (Treffinger et al., 1983). In other words, the promotion of creativity involves both the ability to get ideas and also the willingness to do so. Both these properties are desirable and possible, not only in children of unusually high ability but in all children.

To translate these objectives into practice, Williams (1976c) listed a number of teaching strategies. Adapted for present purposes, these include:

1. giving practice in spotting paradoxes (including inconsistencies and apparent contradictions),
2. training children to notice discrepancies (gaps and missing links),
3. helping children to see analogies (relationships, implications, and so on),
4. helping children to develop skill in searching for and obtaining information,
5. helping children to overcome the effects of habit (breaking out of the straightjacket of conventional thinking),

6. giving children opportunities to engage in visualizing (seeing a problem from a new angle),
7. encouraging children to carry out intuitive thinking (making an informed guess, or following a hunch),
8. fostering communication (both skills and willingness),
9. showing children how to learn from mistakes,
10. helping children to accept change and novelty, and
11. helping children to tolerate ambiguity.

These strategies involve more than simply knowledge and abilities. For example, numbers 7, 10, and 11 require flexibility, willingness to try something out, and readiness to take a chance. Self-criticism and willingness to risk the possibility of failure are needed for number 9. Number 8 requires the self-confidence necessary to offer new ideas (sometimes seen by others as arrogance), but it is also impossible without willingness on the part of other people to accept solutions offered by the creative individual (i.e., it involves social or interpersonal qualities). Even in the area of abilities, it is apparent that carrying out the steps listed above is not just a matter of divergent thinking. In particular, the first four emphasize that creative problem solving calls for the acquisition of substantial information. The most economical way of acquiring this is through the application of convergent thinking skills. Creativity thus involves an integration of convergent and divergent thinking, of motivation, of self-image, and of interpersonal qualities.

Other writers, such as Torrance, Feldhusen, and Treffinger, have suggested similar guidelines for classroom practice in fostering creativity. These have been summarized by Cropley (1982) and include the following lists of "do's" for teachers:

1. show that you value creativity,
2. encourage children to try out new ideas,
3. show tolerance for "way-out" ideas,
4. avoid forcing predigested solutions on to children,
5. encourage independent thinking,
6. offer constructive criticism,
7. make time and materials available for following up children's ideas,
8. encourage children to be many sided in their outlook, and
9. show that you are yourself flexible, many sided, and interested in creative effort.

The guidelines listed to date are not classroom activities in themselves, but directions of development that should influence planning of lessons, selecting material, organizing its presentation, questioning students and reacting to their answers, and setting and evaluating assignments. In every case it is also important to remember, not only that a skill or ability is involved, but that motivational, personal, and social factors also need to be taken into account.

MORE SPECIFIC ACTIVITIES

Playing with Ideas

The notion of "playing" with ideas has already been mentioned as both a characteristic of highly creative people and also an aid to divergent thinking. Endriss (1982) outlined a series of "games" which can be introduced into classroom instruction in order to "unfreeze" or "warm up" ideas. These games are suitable for use with young children, with older students, and with adults. They seek to foster the emergence of various thinking strategies such as those developed by Kirst and Diekmeyer (1973, pp. 127f):

1. producing (offering a coherent idea or thought),
2. analyzing (precisely defining the content of objects and ideas),
3. elaborating (developing a detailed structure on the basis of guiding principles),
4. pointing up (establishing the decisive, definitive elements of objects and ideas),
5. associating (seeing connections between ideas),
6. constructing (combining ideas or objects to form a specified new product),
7. translating (expressing ideas in different forms, or via different modalities—a word being "translated" into a picture, for example),
8. revising (breaking away from existing relationships among ideas and suggesting new ones), and
9. seeing analogies (recognizing new examples of the familiar).

The games themselves take only a few minutes to carry out and can easily be played as a warm-up before any lesson. It is also possible to introduce activities based on these games into the teaching of a large number of subjects. The activities would then be part of the battery of learning and teaching tactics available to all teachers, and should not be treated as discrete events.

In the case of *producing*, for instance, students could be asked to invent the full name of an association identified only by its initials. The associations need not be real ones, but the names derived from the initials must be meaningful, even if exotic. From the initials NPL, for instance, students could suggest "National Peanut League" or "Nameless Parent Lovers," or "Nonplussed Learning." A game for *analyzing* involves giving students a list of materials (such as glass, wind, light, sand) and asking them to list as many ways as possible in which these could be put to use, even if this use is unknown at present. *Elaboration* might require students to describe an object, after being given only certain basic principles. The object need not exist at present but should be rational and at least theoretically imaginable. An amusing game for *pointing up* might be to have students invent nicknames for famous people (not for mutual acquaintances) that summarize as many as possible of the crucial characteristics which make this person a unique individual.

As an *association* activity, students can be asked to invent as many new expressions as they can (these words must have a meaning, even if the word does not actually exist), by joining all or parts of a short list of key words. For instance, they could be asked to find combinations of any forms of *banana, press,* and *break,* such as "daybreak banana presser" = a person who works in a milk bar and prepares banana juice before the start of the day's work, or "banana press break" = an exclusive news story about bananas. An exercise for *constructing* consists of giving pupils three random stimuli—such as "a piece of leather," the word *long* and the process *eating.* The task is to invent, in as elaborated a form as possible, an object which could incorporate all three, such as a device for making it possible to eat leather in long strips. *Translating* can be encouraged by exercises such as asking students to do a drawing (other than a drawing of someone eating) which captures the essence of a sound such as "yum yum."

An exercise which helps to promote *revising* is to ask pupils to suggest novel uses for a well-known object, the most common examples (see both Torrance's, 1974, and Guilford's, 1967, test batteries) being a tin can, a brick, or an empty bottle. A novel idea for how to use a tin can, for example, would be the example already mentioned of using it as a suit of armour for a mouse, in order to give it a fair chance against the cat! Finally, *seeing analogies* can be promoted by giving students a key word, such as *tree,* and asking them to identify as many objects as possible from outside the plant world which could be said to have tree-like properties. A fairly obvious example would be *stalagmite,* and a somewhat more remote one would be *book* (because they both have leaves).

These examples for fostering various thinking strategies through the use of game-like activities, and thus capitalizing on the connection between creativity and play, are not meant to be exhaustive. On the contrary, they are simply examples intended to stimulate teachers' imaginations. Even more important, they can also be treated, not as specific activities to be taken over wholesale, but as tactics or strategies. For instance, a geography teacher could ask students to locate three cities on the world map, given only five facts about the kinds of clothing people wear there (elaborating). A history teacher could ask students to write down what life would be like in their country if certain fictional events had taken place at a particular time (producing, associating, revising, and constructing).

Classroom Exercises

Until now, either general and abstract principles for fostering creativity in pupils, or broader procedures for stimulating ideas, have been described. The following material provides examples of actual classroom activities. It offers examples and initial suggestions only, and does not constitute an exhaustive list of things that teachers might do. The examples are not sorted or arranged in any way according, for example, to the ages of children for whom they are appropriate, or according to subject areas. Rather, they are meant to prime the ingenuity of educators in devising activities suited to their particular grades and subjects.

Building an Idea Trap. Keeping a scrap book or similar record of ideas is one way of providing opportunities for children to communicate ideas, and for teachers to reinforce them. This record of ideas, which may occur at any time, is an "idea trap." The teacher may then set aside occasional periods for going through idea traps, write proffered ideas on the blackboard, discuss some of them, or show approval of particularly clever ideas. The idea trap period may function as a nonevaluated period.

Sounds and Images. Openness to experience, sensitivity to one's own sensory processes, and similar activities can be encouraged by playing unusual or difficult-to-recognize sounds on a tape recorder and asking students to imagine what the sounds might be. They can then draw pictures that seem to contain the meaning of the sounds in a pictorial form, write stories based on the sounds, or represent them in dance. This kind of activity can also serve as the basis for a classroom discussion of the difficulties and problems associated with having ideas and imagining things.

Story Writing. Several of the activities already described can be integrated into story-writing sessions. Children may take a number of ideas from their idea traps and weave them together into a story, or they may express their playful ideas in the form of a story. Stories can then be read out in class, put together, and "published" in a class magazine.

Improving Objects. The teacher may introduce a toy (or some more age-appropriate object) into the classroom and invite students to indicate how it could be improved. Again, opportunities are provided for a delay of evaluation, recognition, the fostering of worthwhile ideas, guided self-evaluation, and group brainstorming.

Activities Derived from Creativity Tests

One result of recent interest in fostering creativity has been the emergence of so-called "creativity" tests. Apart from their use as tests, however, materials such as those developed by Guilford and Torrance provide valuable suggestions for classroom activities likely to foster divergent thinking. The present section outlines a number of these, which students have found interesting and exciting. The outlines provided here are intended for use, not in testing creativity, but in fostering it.

The activities are both verbal and nonverbal in content. They may be used with students over a wide age range, from early grades to university level. A general set of instructions can be used to introduce all of them, although additional instructions are needed for each specific activity. Some changes may be made for children of differing age levels. Generally the teacher tells students:

> I want to see how good you are at making up interesting, unusual, and clever ideas. Remember it is interesting, clever, and unusual ideas that we are concerned with in this exercise. Don't be afraid to suggest ideas that are a bit 'way-out.' The main thing is to try to think of ideas that nobody else in the class will think of. Try to show how original and creative you can be with your answers.

In the case of the exercises requiring verbal answers, responses may be written down individually by each student, or they may be called out aloud and written on the blackboard. In this latter case, the teacher may discuss to what extent the response offered is interesting, unusual, and creative. Some activities may be carried out by individual students at their own desks, or students might use the exercises as the basis for brainstorming or synectics groups.

Seeing Problems. In this activity, the students' job is to make up problems that might arise in connection with some situation or object. For example, they could be asked, after being given the general introduction outlined above, to make up as many interesting and unusual problems as they can which might arise in connection with a tree growing in somebody's backyard. An example of a relatively creative response is the following: "What sort of license would be needed to rent nesting space to birds?"

Uses. In this exercise, the students' job is to think of as many interesting and unusual cases as possible for a common object such as a tin can.

Common responses showing low levels of creativity will include suggestions like "saucepan," "door stopper," or "shower head." The example of the suit of armor for a mouse is uncommon. Any other common object, say, a brick, can be substituted for a tin can.

Consequences. The Consequences activity requires students to think of possible results of unlikely events. They might be asked to make up consequences of a situation in which it started raining all over the world and never stopped. Relatively inventive and unusual responses include: "The cost of real estate on mountain tops would rise sharply" and "It would cost a great deal more to rent a diving suit." Alternative situations are limited only by the teacher's inventiveness. Students could be asked the consequences if the earth were covered by a mist, if the clouds had strings hanging from them, if people lost all feelings for each other, and many more.

Naming Things. The students are asked to give the names of as many things as they can think of which have a certain property—for example, things that are round. The idea is to try to go beyond common round things like buttons or plates, or the sun, and to think of things which could accurately be described as round but which would not normally be so described. One example is "the mind of a well-educated person." Again, the property nominated need not be round, but square, pretty, noisy, or any adjective.

Using Shapes. The activities just described have all involved verbal responses. However, it is also possible to design exercises in which the responses are nonverbal. Using Shapes is one such activity. In this exercise, students are given previously prepared paper or cardboard shapes, such as an egg-shaped piece of paper or cardboard. (The shapes may also be provided in the form of gummed paper, so that, instead of being copied, they can be stuck directly onto the drawing paper.) The task is to place the particular shape anywhere on the paper and then incorporate it into a drawing. For example, one grade-4 boy who was given a kidney-shaped piece of sticky paper glued it at the top of his page with the slight U-shaped opening downwards, and subsequently drew a matador whose hat was formed by the shape provided.

Circles. The students are given a large sheet of drawing paper which has been covered with circles of approximately 1½″ diameter. The exercise involves making up as many interesting and unusual drawings as possible which incorporate one or more of the circles as an integral part. In one example of a relatively inventive response, a student used two of the circles as the nostril openings and drew a nose as it would look to a fly perched on a person's upper lip.

Finishing Drawings. The students are given a sheet of drawing paper containing a number of lines that may or may not be joined together, may be curved or straight, and may be of the same or differing colors. The task is to incorporate these lines into a completed drawing. In this exercise, as in previous ones, the general introduction at the beginning of the section should be used to explain to students the nature of the task. In all activities requiring drawings as responses, it is wise to ask students to give a title to their drawings. Otherwise, it is not always easy to grasp what has been drawn, especially if the responses are particularly original.

A third kind of activity involves a mixture of verbal and nonverbal procedures. This activity is useful in emphasizing that ideas may be expressed in ways other than words. Activities of a mixed kind have the additional advantage that they emphasize the possibility of combining verbal and nonverbal methods of expression in thinking divergently.

Symbol Production. This activity involves verbal stimuli and nonverbal responses. In the introduction the students are asked to draw symbols representing words. For example, they could be asked to draw an airplane taking off. The idea is not to draw an actual aeroplane but to symbolize it. An example would be a horizontal line with, just above it, a line parallel to it suddenly turning and running upwards towards the top of the page, with an arrowhead placed at its end. The horizontal line symbolizes the ground, and the ascending line symbolizes an airplane moving parallel to the ground in the early stages of the takeoff and then climbing into the sky.

Asking Questions. This exercise involves showing the students a picture, or sketch, or even a cartoon of some scene, preferably involving people. The exercise is to make up as many questions as possible about what is happening. The idea is not to ask questions whose answers are immediately apparent from looking at the drawing, but to ask inventive and original questions which refer to incidents that have preceded the picture, that follow it, that are going on elsewhere, and that are, in other ways, not requests for simple facts about the picture.

In all of these exercises, some difficulties will usually be experienced in the initial stages in getting students to produce ideas freely. They are too accustomed to emphasis on correct ideas and will look for more information concerning how they "should" go about completing the exercises. If the teacher shows that it is their own ideas that are required, and urges them to be inventive and creative, students will soon begin to enjoy the activities and to generate many ideas. Teachers can facilitate this process by reading answers aloud or showing drawings to the whole class. The exercises give teachers an opportunity to show their personal interest in ideas and so serve a double function in that they help to give children practice in producing ideas and also to establish a classroom climate favorable to their production.

IMPLICATIONS FOR CURRICULUM

Recent Increasing One-Sidedness

One effect of the conditions of modern life has been an increasing tendency for schooling to concentrate on the kinds of thinking needed for interaction with a complex technology. As a result, there has been increasing emphasis on strictly logical, goal-oriented thinking, and decreasing emphasis on the social and emotional processes through which students gain experience in expressing their feelings, experiencing their own emotions, and relating to other people. This increasing one-sidedness in the psychological processes fostered in schools means that they may well be tending to strengthen rather than oppose alienating forces seen to be at work in modern life. Two kinds of estrangement are described by educational writers: estrangement from other people, and even more importantly, estrangement from aspects of oneself. It is as though people are learning two ways of relating to their worlds, one which is intellectual and one which is emotional. The latter kind of functioning may well be in danger of being overwhelmed by the former: A dissociation between intellectual and emotional life may be taking place. The consequences of this state of affairs for creative thinking have already been spelled out in Chapter 4. In a nutshell, any tendency for schools to foster purely convergent, abstract verbal reasoning at the expense of divergent thinking would not only involve one-sidedness but would also be highly likely to inhibit creativity.

The Need for Balance

Schools are charged with responsibility for transmitting the basic skills students will need in order to fit into society when they become adults, including the skills needed in order to make a living. The importance of this task should not be overlooked by the proponents of reform. Our society depends upon the steady supply of people who can help to maintain its complex social and technological structures. However, important as these aspects of education are, they are not its only functions. A balance is needed between the requirements of the technological society and the spiritual, emotional, and social needs of human beings, both individually and collectively. There is a danger that schools will become overly one-sided in the kinds of thinking they foster, with the result that they may neglect aspects of thinking vital to creativity. As a result, encouragement of daring, innovative, original, and free-ranging thinking requires a more balanced understanding of the intellectual, emotional, and motivational aspects of thinking and learning. Consequently, teachers need to seek ways in which they can extend curricula, in order to provide opportunities for creative thinking.

"Aesthetic" Education

One way in which this might be achieved is through the greater development of "aesthetic" education. This kind of education places greater emphasis on the emotional and affective sides of life through the teaching of art, music, and related activities. Aesthetic education is more than simply an opportunity to sharpen children's appreciation of artistic works. It also provides an opportunity for expression of personal feelings, for the production of ideas, and for experiencing and expressing values. Along with these come opportunities for evaluating one's own work on the basis of internal rather than external criteria. Finally, aesthetic education has great potential for increasing students' opportunities for communicating with other people. Thus, it can be seen as a potent tool for the fostering of creativity in the classroom.

However, aesthetic education is often seen as merely a setting in which to develop children's aesthetic sensibility so that they learn to enjoy the artistic traditions of the society. This is a very desirable goal, of course, but it should not be the sole aim of aesthetic education. It is important that it also involve strong elements of expressive and innovative thinking, of positive evaluation of children's own ideas, and of internal locus of evaluation. This means that it should contain many opportunities for students to attempt their own imaginative and creative products in periods devoted to "practical" activities. However, these periods need to be something more than simply breaks from the usual classroom routine, in which children can daub paints without restrictions or whisper together while the teacher plays records of the "greats"! Periods devoted to aesthetic education offer exceptional opportunities for establishing a climate favorable to the production of ideas, for reinforcing such ideas, for demonstrating innovative and free-ranging thinking, and for encouraging guided self-evaluation.

Unfortunately, many teachers in the area report that achievement of these goals is greatly hindered by the fact that society stereotypes art, music, and similar pursuits as recreational activities (which of course they are) alone, not as integral aspects of both life and school curriculum in which valuable thinking skills can be fostered. As a result, students bring negative attitudes into their lessons, curriculum planners and timetable organizers relegate aesthetic education to odd corners of school schedules, and even teachers in the area accept many of these negative stereotypes, themselves feeling like interlopers or like "frills." What is seen here is the existence of a very broad unfavorable "climate" encompassing, not just classrooms, but the whole educational structure and the society at large. This climate is unfavorable to the full development of aesthetic education and to its full contribution to the fostering of creativity in the classroom.

"Play" Education

Getzels and Jackson (1962), Hudson (1966), and Graham et al. (1989) stressed the value of play and fantasy in creative thinking. Adopting a psychoanalytic approach, Smith and Carlsson (1989) defined *creativity* as the ability to communicate with one's own subjective world. Play makes this possible, because it is not bound by reality constraints (see Sappington & Farrar, 1982) and because, during play, social barriers are lowered. Bruner (1975), Piaget (1962), and Sutton-Smith (1967) each also emphasized the importance of play in children, and especially its role in fostering their creativity. Play does not seem to serve any basic needs (such as obtaining food) but, despite this, children persistently engage in it (Berlyne, 1968). Furthermore, a number of psychological studies have shown that play activities are related to the degree of creativity shown by children. It seems that, in play, children try out behaviors that would not normally appear, for example, because pressure for correctness or for social acceptability are eased during play. When they play, children can also deal with the external world in purely personal ways, turning the locus of evaluation inwards. They can give their fantasy freer reign. Thus, play provides a situation in which many of the social and emotional blocks to creative thinking are not present, and permits many of the creativity-facilitating activities mentioned in earlier chapters.

Bruner (1972) in particular stressed that, in play, the need for strictly logical correctness can be relaxed, the possible or fantastic taken into consideration, and the locus of evaluation moved inwards, because, in play, "the rules" can be ignored. Play permits greater flexibility because, when strict correctness is not required, many more alternatives can be considered. In psychoanalytic theory (e.g., Freud, Kris, Kubie) the relationship between creativity and such relaxing of the rules is greatly emphasized (see, among others, Stein & Stein, 1984). For this reason, play looks to offer an important opportunity for fostering creativity. This notion is supported by the fact that several studies have shown that creativity test scores are enhanced by play-like conditions of administration. Bloom (1985) found that "play" with a musical instrument in early childhood was an essential prerequisite for later musical creativity.

Not all children play freely and imaginatively. Freeman (1990) drew attention to cross-cultural studies which showed that play is uncommon in some societies, and argued that, even within a given society, children differ substantially from one another in the amount and quality of play. It has been shown that play activities are affected by adult models and by the provision of play-facilitating conditions. Rosen (1974) and Graham et al. (1989), for instance, demonstrated that observation of appropriate adult models increased play activity among children. In other words, teachers are able to influence the amount children play, and thus have at their disposal an important tool for fostering creativity—one which many children engage in naturally and for which they show high levels of intrinsic motivation. At the same time, teachers have the power to guide play in ways that will increase creative thinking. To put it plainly, play seems to offer an excellent device for the fostering of classroom—and indeed real-life—creativity.

Unfortunately, it is doubtful whether adequate advantage is taken of this state of affairs. Play and work are frequently regarded as mutually irreconcilable. School principals, superintendents, and parents are likely to disapprove strongly if classroom activities have too much of the air of play about them (Elkind, 1981). Even children themselves may feel guilty and uneasy and may complain that they are not learning properly. Sometimes, teachers will thus actually have to coax children into playing. As Freeman (1990) pointed out, they may have to help the children overcome play difficulties, for instance, by starting them off with simpler, even babyish, toys. At the lower age levels, the disposition to play creatively can be fostered in many simple ways: telling stories, inventing games, dressing up, building things out of packing cases, and so on. As was the case with aesthetic education, society has not yet accepted the validity of play and play-like procedures as legitimate components of the learning process. It is important to add, as a kind of footnote, that what is being advocated here is not abandonment of all curricular elements except art, music, and play! The point is that curricula show the same imbalance and one-sidedness that has been described in, for example, the conceptualization of intelligence, and that creative thinking processes suffer as a result. What is needed is a better balance, not a different kind of imbalance.

System Inertia—The Task for Individual Teachers

The suggestions made here are not necessarily novel. A large number of educational workers probably accept in principle many of the ideas advanced both in the present section and in the text as a whole. However, the educational structure is a large and complex one and is subject to close scrutiny by society. Consequently, there is a great deal of inertia in the system. Furthermore, excessive enthusiasm and unduly hasty change, without careful prior analysis of the details, implications, probable outcomes, and likely drawbacks, have greatly increased this inertia and even distrust of change. A certain conservatism in considering whether to make wholesale changes in a system so complex, and at the same time so important to society, as education seems to be justified, so that administrators, planners, and legislators cannot be blamed for exercising caution. As a result, a special responsibility devolves upon individual teachers to recognize their role at the level in the educational structure at which change is most readily effected. However, it is important that they are well informed, and that they exercise discretion, sense, and judgment.

FURTHER READING

Henslowe, S.A. (1986). *Handbook of instructional materials for education of the gifted and talented.* Edmonton, Canada: Alberta Education Planning Services.

Herr, J.A., & Libby, Y.R. (1990). *Creative resources for the early childhood classroom.* Albany, NY: Delmar.

Mallis, J. (1982). *Diamonds in the dust—discover and develop your child's gift.* Austin, TX: Multi Media.

Mayesky, M.E. (1990). *Creative activities for young children.* Albany, NY: Delmar.

Taylor, C.W. (Ed.). (1972). *Climate of creativity.* New York: Oxford.

References

Altshuller, G.S. (1984). *Creativity as an exact science*. New York: Gordon and Breach.

Amabile, T.M. (1983). *The social psychology of creativity*. New York: Springer.

Amabile, T.M., Goldfarb, P., & Brackfield, S.C. (1990). Social influences on creativity: Evaluation coaction, surveillance. *Creativity Research Journal, 3*, 6–21.

Ammon, G. (1974). *Gruppendynamik der Kreativität*. Munich: Kindler.

Andreasen, N.C. (1987). Creativity and mental illness: Prevalence rates in writers and their first degree relatives. *American Journal of Psychiatry, 144*, 1288–1292.

Anthony, E.J. (1987). Risk, vulnerability and resilience: An overview. In E.J. Anthony & B.J. Cohen (Eds.), *The invulnerable child* (pp. 3–48). New York: Guilford Press.

Barron, F.X. (1963). *Creativity and psychological health*. New York: Van Nostrand.

Barron, F.X. (1969). *Creative person and creative process*. New York: Holt, Rinehart and Winston.

Barron, F.X., & Harrington, D.M. (1981). Creativity, intelligence and personality. *Annual Review of Psychology, 32*, 439–476.

Basadur, M., Wakabayashi, M, & Graen, G. (1990). Problem solving styles, and attitudes towards divergent thinking before and after training. *Creativity Research Journal , 3*, 22–32.

Bayer, A.E., & Folger, J. (1966). Some correlates of a citation measure of productivity in science. *Sociology of Education, 39*, 381–390.

Belcher, T.L. (1975). Modeling original divergent responses: An initial investigation. *Journal of Educational Psychology, 67*, 351–358.

Berlyne, D.E. (1968). Laughter, humor and play. In G. Lindzey & E. Aronson (Eds.), *Handbook of social psychology* (2nd ed., Vol. III, pp. 795–852). Reading, MA: Addison Wesley.

Besemer, S.B., & Treffinger, D.J. (1981). Analysis of creative products: Review and synthesis. *Journal of Creative Behavior, 16*, 68–73.

Biermann, K.-R. (1985). Über Stigmata der Kreativität bei Mathematikern des 17. bis 19. Jahrhunderts. *Rostocker Mathematik Kolloquium, 27*, 5–22.

Biggs, J.B. (1973). Content to process. *Australian Journal of Education, 17*, 225–238.

Bloom, B.S. (1971). Mastery learning and its implications for curriculum development. In E.W. Eisner (Ed.), *Confronting curriculum reform*. Boston, Little Brown.

Bloom, B.S. (1976). *Human characteristics and school learning.* New York: McGraw Hill.

Bloom, B.S. (1985). *Developing talent in young people.* New York: Ballantine.

de Bono, E. (1971). *The uses of lateral thinking.* Hardmondsworth, UK: Penguin.

Brown, R.A. (1977). Creativity, discovery and science. *Journal of Chemical Education, 5,* 720–724.

Bruner, J.S. (1962). The conditions of creativity. In H. Gruber, G. Terrell, & M. Wertheimer (Eds.), *Contemporary approaches to creative thinking* (pp. 1–30). New York: Atherton.

Bruner, J.S. (1972). The nature and uses of immaturity. *American Psychologist, 27,* 1–28.

Bruner, J.S. (1975). Child development: Play is serious business. *Psychology Today, 8,* 80–83.

Calvi, G. (1966). *Il problem psicologico della creatività.* Milan: Ceschina.

Campbell, D.T. (1960). Blind variation and selective retention in creative thought as in other knowledge processes. *Psychological Review, 67,* 380–400.

Cattell, R.B. (1963). Theory of fluid and crystallized intelligence: A critical experiment. *Journal of Educational Psychology, 54,* 1–22.

Cattell, R.B., & Butcher, H.J. (1968). *The prediction of achievement and creativity.* New York: Bobbs-Merrill.

Clement, J. (1989). Learning via model construction and criticism: Protocoll evidence on sources of creativity in science. In J.A. Glover, R.R. Ronning, & C.R. Reynolds (Eds.), *Handbook of creativity* (pp. 341–388). New York: Plenum.

Cohen, L. (1989). A continuum of adaptive creative behaviors. *Creativity Research Journal, 2,* 169–183.

Coleman, J.S. (1966). *Equality of educational opportunity.* Washington, DC: U.S. Govt. Printing Office.

Covington, M.V. (1967, August). *Productive thinking and a cognitive curriculum.* Invited paper presented at the symposium Studies of the Inquiry Process, Problems of Theory, Description and Teaching, American Psychological Association, Washington, DC.

Cox, C.M. (1926). *Genetic studies of genius: The early mental traits of three hundred geniuses.* Palo Alto, CA: Stanford University Press.

Cropley, A.J. (1967a). *Creativity.* London: Longmans.

Cropley, A.J. (1967b). Divergent thinking and science specialists. *Nature, 215,* 671–672.

Cropley, A.J. (1969). Creativity, intelligence and intellectual style. *Australian Journal of Education, 13,* 3–7.

Cropley, A.J. (1972). A five-year longitudinal study of the validity of creativity tests. *Developmental Psychology, 6,* 119–124.

Cropley, A.J.. (1973). Creativity and culture. *Educational Trends, 8,* 19–27.

Cropley, A.J. (1974). Lifelong education: A Panacea for all educational ills? *Australian Journal of Education, 18,* 1–15.

Cropley, A.J. (1981). Hochbegabung und Kreativität: Eine Herausforderung für die Schule. In W.H. Wieczerkowski & H. Wagner (Eds.), *Das hochbegabte Kind* (pp. 68–81). Düsseldorf: Schwann.

Cropley, A.J. (1982). *Kreativität und Erziehung*. Munich: Reinhardt.

Cropley, A.J. (1990). Creativity and mental health. *Creativity Research Journal, 3,* 167–178.

Cropley, A.J. (1991). Improving intelligence: Fostering creativity in everyday settings. In H.A.H. Rowe (Ed.), *Intelligence: Reconceptualization and measurement* (pp. 267–280). Hillsdale, NJ: Erlbaum.

Cropley, A.J., & Feuring, E. (1971). Training creativity in young children. *Developmental Psychology, 4,* 105.

Cropley, A.J., & Sikand, J.S. (1973). Creativity and schizophrenia. *Journal of Consulting and Clinical Psychology, 40,* 462–468.

Dansky, J.L. (1980). Make-believe: A mediator of the relationship between play and associative fluency. *Child Development, 51,* 576–579.

Davis, G.A., & Scott, J.A. (1971). *Training creative thinking*. New York: Holt, Reinhart and Winston.

Dellas, M., & Gaier, E.L. (1970). Identification of creativity: The individual. *Psychological Bulletin, 73,* 55–73.

Drevdahl, J.E., & Cattell, R.B. (1958). Personality and creativity in artists and writers. *Journal of Clinical Psychology, 14,* 107–111.

Eiduson, B.T. (1958). Artist and non-artist: A comparative study. *Journal of Personality, 26,* 13–28.

Elkind, D. (1981). *The hurried child*. Reading, MA: Addison-Wesley.

Ellis, H.A. (1926). *A study of British genius*. New York: Houghton Mifflin.

Endriss, L. (1982). *Entwicklung und Auswirkung eines Kreativitätstrainings— Förderung des spielerischen Denkens bei jungen Erwachsenen*. Unpublished masters thesis, University of Hamburg.

Facaoaru, C. (1985). *Kreativität in Wissenschaft und Technik*. Bern: Huber.

Facaoaru, C., & Bittner, R. (1987). Kognitionspsychologische Ansätze der Hochbegabungsdiagnostik. *Zeitschrift für Differentielle und Diagnostische Psychologie, 8*(3), 193–205.

Farisha, B. (1978). Mental imagery and creativity: Review and speculation. *Journal of Mental Imagery, 2,* 209–238.

Feldhusen, J.F., & Treffinger, D.J. (1980). *Creative thinking and problem solving in gifted education*. Dubuque, IO: Kendall/Hunt Publishing Co.

Franklin, B.S., & Richards, P.N. (1977). Effects on children's divergent thinking abilities of a period of direct teaching for divergent production. *British Journal of Educational Psychology, 47,* 66–70.

Freeman, J. (1983). Emotional problems of the gifted child. *Journal of Child Psychology and Psychiatry, 24,* 481–485.

Freeman, J. (1990). The early development and education of highly able young children. *European Journal for High Ability, 1,* 165–171.

Freud, S. (1910). *Leonardo da Vinci: A study in psychosexuality*. New York: Random House.

Fromm, E. (1980). *Greatness and limitations of Freud's thought*. New York: New American Library.

Gallagher, J.J. (1986). The conservation of intellectual resources. In A.J. Cropley, K.K. Urban, H. Wagner, & W.H. Wieczerkowski (Eds.), *Giftedness: A continuing worldwide challenge* (pp. 21–30). New York: Trillium.

Gardner, H. (1983). *Frames of mind: The theory of multiple intelligences.* New York: Basic Books.

Gardner, H. (1988). Creativity: An interdisciplinary perspective. *Creativity Research Journal, 1*, 8–26.

Getzels, J.W., & Jackson, P.W. (1962). *Creativity and intelligence.* New York: John Wiley.

Ghiselin, B. (Ed.). (1952). *The creative process.* Berkeley and Los Angeles: University of California Press.

Gibson, J., & Light, P. (1967). Intelligence among university scientists. *Nature, 213,* 441–443.

Glover, J., & Gary, A.L. (1976). Procedures to increase some aspects of creativity. *Journal of Applied Behavior Analysis, 9*, 79–84.

Golann, S.E. (1963). Psychological study of creativity. *Psychological Bulletin, 60,* 548–565.

Goleman, D. (1980, February). 1528 little geniuses and how they grew. *Psychology Today*, pp. 28–43.

Gordon, W.J. (1961). *Synectics.* New York: Harper Bros.

Graham, B., Sawyers, J., & Debord, K.B. (1989). Teacher's creativity, playfulness, and style of interaction. *Creativity Research Journal, 2*, 41–50.

Guilford, J.P. (1950). Creativity. *American Psychologist, 5*, 444–454.

Guilford, J.P. (1962). Factors that aid and hinder creativity. *Teacher's College Record, 63*, 380–392.

Guilford, J.P. (1967). *The nature of human intelligence.* New York: McGraw-Hill.

Hadamard, J. (1945). *An essay on the psychology of invention in the mathematical field.* Princeton, NJ: University Press.

Haddon, F.A., & Lytton, H. (1968). Teaching approach and the development of divergent thinking abilities in primary schools. *British Journal of Educational Psychology, 38*, 171–180.

Hammer, E.F. (1964). Creativity and feminine ingredients in young male artists. *Perceptual and Motor Skills, 19*, 414.

Hare, A.P. (1982). *Creativity in small groups.* Beverly Hills, CA: Sage.

Hartmann, H. (1958). *Ego psychology and the problem of adaptation.* New York: International Universities Press.

Hassenstein, M. (1988). *Bausteine zu einer Naturgeschichte der Intelligenz.* Stuttgart: Deutsche Verlags-Anstalt.

Heinelt, G. (1974). *Kreative Lehrer—kreative Schüler.* Frieburg: Herder.

Helson, R. (1966). Personality of women with imagination and artistic interests: The role of masculinity, originality, and other characteristics in their creativity. *Journal of Personality, 34*, 1–25.

Helson, R. (1983). Creative mathematicians. In R.S. Albert (Ed.), *Genius and eminence: The social psychology of creativity and exceptional achievement* (pp. 311–330). Elmsford, NY: Pergamon.

Helson, R., & Crutchfield, R.S. (1970). The creative researcher and the average Ph.D. *Journal of Consulting and Clinical psychology, 34*, 250–257.

Hendrickson, L. (1986). A longitudinal study of precocity in music. In A.J. Cropley, K.K. Urban, H. Wagner, & W.H. Wieczerkowski (Eds.), *Giftedness: A continuing worldwide challenge* (pp. 192–203). New York: Trillium.

Hennesey, B.A., & Amabile, T.M. (1988). Storytelling: A method for assessing children's creativity. *Journal of Creative Behavior, 22,* 235–246.

Henslowe, S.A. (1986). *Handbook of instructional materials for education of the gifted and talented.* Edmonton, Canada: Alberta Education Planning Services.

Herrmann, W. (1987). *Auswirkungen verschiedener Fußball-Trainingsstile auf Leistungsmotivation.* Unpublished master's thesis, University of Hamburg.

Hitchfield, E. (1973). *In search of promise.* London: Longman.

Hocevar, D. (1980). Intelligence, divergent thinking and creativity, *Intelligence, 4,* 25–40.

Hocevar, D. (1981). Measurement of creativity: Review and critique. *Journal of Personality Assessment, 45,* 450–464.

Holden, C. (1987). Creativity and the troubled mind. *Psychology Today, 21(4),* 9–10.

Hoomes, E.W. (1984). Future problem solving. *G/T/C, 7,* 15–18.

Horn, J.L. (1988, August). *Major issues before us now and for the next few decades.* Paper presented at Seminar on Intelligence, Melbourne, Australia.

Horowitz, F.D., & O'Brien, M. (1986). Gifted and talented children: State of knowledge and direction for research. *American Psychologist, 41,* 1147–1152.

Houtz, J.C., Jambor, S.O., Cifone, A., & Lewis, C.D. (1989). Locus of evaluation control, task directions, and type of problem effects on creativity. *Creativity Research Journal, 2,* 118–125.

Howieson, N. (1981). A longitudinal study of creativity—1965–1975. *Journal of Creative Behavior, 15(2),* 117–134.

Howieson, N. (1984, August). *Is Western Australia neglecting the creative potential of its youth?* Paper presented at the 1984 Annual Conference of the Australian Psychological Society, Perth, Australia.

Hudson, L. (1966). *Contrary imaginations.* London: Methuen.

Hudson, L. (1968). *Frames of mind.* London: Methuen.

Humphreys, L.G. (1985). A conceptualization of intellectual giftedness. In F.D. Horowitz & M. O'Brien (Eds.), *The gifted and talented: Developmental perspectives* (pp. 331–360). Washington, DC: American Psychological Association.

Inhelder, B., & Piaget, J. (1958). *The growth of logical thinking from childhood to adolescence.* New York: Basic Books.

Jamison, K.R. (1989). Manic-depressive illness and accomplishment: Creativity, leadership and social class. In F.K. Goodwin & K.R. Jamison (Eds.), *Manic-depressive illness.* Oxford: Oxford University Press.

Jencks, C., Smith, M., Acland, H., Bone, M.J., Cohen, D., Gintis, H., Heyns, B., & Michelson, S. (1972). *Inequality: The social determinants of success.* New York: Basic Books.

Jenkins, J.J. & Paterson, D.G. (1961). *Studies in individual differences.* New York: Appleton-Century-Crofts.

Juda, A. (1949). The relationship between highest mental capacity and psychic abnormalities. *American Journal of Psychiatry, 106,* 296–307.

Kerry, T. (1981). *Teaching bright pupils in mixed ability classes.* London: Macmillan.

Kirst, W., & Diekmeyer, U. (1973). *Kreativitätstraining*. Reinbek bei Hamburg: Rowohlt.

Klix, F., & van der Meer, E. (1986). Mathematical giftedness: Its nature and possible early identification. In A.J. Cropley, K.K. Urban, H. Wagner, & W.H. Wieczerkowski (Eds.). *Giftedness: A continuing worldwide challenge* (pp. 244–245). New York: Trillum.

Kneller, G.F. (1965). *The art and science of creativity*. New York: Holt, Rinehart, & Winston.

König, F. (1986). Kreativit.ätsdiagnostik als essentieller Bestandteil der Intelligenzdiagnostik. *Diagnostica, 32*, 345–357.

Krampen, G., Freilinger, J., & Wilmes, L. (1988). Kreativitätstest für Vorschul- und Schulkinder (KVS): Testentwicklung, Handanweisung, Testheft. *Trierer Psychologische Berichte, 15*(Whole No. 7).

Krause, R. (1972). *Kreativität*. Munich: Goldmann.

Krause, R. (1977). *Produktives Denken bei Kindern*. Weinheim: Beltz.

Krystal, H. (1988). On some roots of creativity. *Psychiatric Clinics of North America, 11*, 475–491.

Langer, E., Hatem M., Joss., J., & Howell, M. (1989). Conditional teaching and mindful learning. The role of uncertainty in education. *Creativity Research Journal, 2*, 139–150.

Lehman, H.C. (1953). *Age and achievement*. Princeton, NJ: Princeton University Press.

Lehman, H.C., & Witty, P.A. (1931). Scientific eminence and church membership. *Scientific Monthly, 33*, 544–549.

Lombroso, C. (1891). *The man of genius*. London: Scott.

Lowenfeld, V. (1957). *Creativity and mental growth*. New York: Macmillan.

MacKinnon, D.W. (1965). Personality and the realization of creative potential. *American Psychologist, 20*, 273–281.

MacKinnon, D.W. (1983). Creative architects. In R.S. Albert (Ed.), *Genius and eminence: The social psychology of creativity and exceptional achievement* (pp. 291–301). Elmsford, NY: Pergamon.

Maltzmann, I., Simon, S., Raskin, D., & Licht, I. (1960). Experimental studies in the training of originality. *Psychological Monographs, 6*.

Mansfield, R.S., Busse, T.V., & Krepelka, E.J. (1978). The effectiveness of creativity training. *Review of Educational Research, 48*, 517–536.

Marjoram, T. (1988). *Teaching able children*. London: Kogan Page.

Maslany, G.W. (1973). *Predictive validity of intellectual tests*. Unpublished doctoral dissertation, University of Calgary.

Maslow, A.H. (1954). *Motivation and personality*. New York: Harper.

Maslow, A.H. (1971). *The farther reaches of human nature*. New York: Viking Press.

Matyushkin, A.M. (1990). A Soviet perspective on giftedness and creativity. *European Journal for High Ability, 1*, 72–75.

McGreevy, J. (1982). *My book of things and stuff. An interest questionnaire for young children*. Mansfield, CT: Creative Learning Press.

McLaren, R. (in press). The dark side of creativity. *Creativity Research Journal*.

McLeod, J., & Cropley, A.J. (1989). *Fostering academic excellence*. Oxford: Pergamon.

McNeil, T.F. (1971). Prebirth and postbirth influence on the relationship between creative ability and recorded mental illness. *Journal of Personality, 39,* 391–406.

Mednick, S.A. (1962). The associative basis of creativity. *Psychological Review, 69,* 220–232.

Mehlhorn, H.-G., Chalupsky, J., Kauke, M., Lorf-Kolker, M., Mehlhorn, G., & Paetzold, G. (1988). *Persönlichkeitsentwicklung Hochbegabter.* Berlin: Volk und Wissen Volkseigener Verlag.

Meinberger, U. (1977). *Test zum divergenten Denken (Kreativität) für 4. bis 6. Klassen (TDK 4–6).* Weinheim: Beltz.

Milgram, R.M. (1990). Creativity: An idea whose time has come and gone? In M.A. Runco & R.S. Albert (Eds.), *Theories of creativity* (pp. 215–233). Newbury Park, CA: Sage Publications.

Moore, O.K. (1961). Orthographic symbols and the pre-school child—a new approach. In E.P. Torrance (Ed.), *New educational ideas: Second Minnesota Conference on Gifted Children.* Minneapolis: University of Minnesota Press.

Motamedi, K. (1982). Extending the concept of creativity. *Journal of Creative Behavior, 16,* 75–88.

Necka, E. (1986). On the nature of creative talent. In A.J. Cropley, K.K. Urban, H. Wagner, & W.H. Wieczerkowski (Eds.), *Giftedness: A continuing worldwide challenge* (pp. 131–140). New York: Trillium.

Nicholls, J.G. (1972). Creativity in the person who will never produce anything original and useful: the concept of creativity as a normally distributed trait. *American Psychologist, 27,* 717–727.

Obuche, N.M. (1986). The ideal pupil as perceived by Nigerian (Igbo) teachers and Torrance's creativity personality. *International Review of Education, 32,* 191–196.

Okuda, S.M., Runco, M.A., & Berger, D.E. (1990). *Creativity and the finding and solving of real world problems.* Manuscript submitted for publication.

Ornstein, J.A. (1961). New recruits for science. *Parents' Magazine, 36,* 101–103.

Osborn, A.F. (1953). *Applied imagination.* New York: Scribner.

Parloff, M.D., & Handlon, J.H. (1964). The influence of criticalness on creative problem solving. *Psychiatry, 27,* 17–27.

Perkins, D.N. (1981). *The mind's best work.* .Cambridge, MA: Harvard University Press.

Petersen, S. (1989). *Motivation von Laienautoren.* Unpublished masters thesis, University of Hamburg.

Piaget, J. (1962). *Play, dreams, and imitation in childhood.* New York: Norton.

Rein, W. (Ed.). (1904). *Enzykopädisches Handbuch der Pädagogik.* Langensalza: Bayer and Sons.

Renzulli, J.S. (1977). *The enrichment triad model: A guide for developing defensible programs for the gifted and talented.* Wethersfield, CT: Creative Learning Press.

Renzulli, J.S. (1982). What makes a problem real: Stalking the illusive meaning of qualitative differences in gifted education. *Gifted Child Quarterly, 26,* 747–756.

Renzulli, J.S. (1984). The triad/revolving door system: A research-based approach to identification and programming for the gifted and talented. *Gifted Child Quarterly, 28,* 163–171.

Renzulli, J.S., Reis, S.M., & Smith, L.H. (1981, May). The revolving door model: A new way of identifying the gifted. *Phi Delta Kappan,* pp. 648–649.

Richards, R., & Kinney, D.K. (1990) Mood swings and creativity. *Creativity Research Journal, 3,* 202–217.

Richards, R., Kinney, D.K., Bennet, M., & Merzel, A.P.C. (1988). Assessing everyday creativity: Characteristics of the Lifetime Creativity Scales and validation with three large samples. *Journal of Personality and Social Psychology, 54,* 476–485.

Richards, R., Kinney, D.K., Lunde, I., Bennet, M., & Merzel, A.P.C. (1988). Creativity in manic-depressives, cyclothymes, their normal relatives, and control subjects. *Journal of Abnormal Psychology, 9,* 281–288.

Rimm, S., & Davis, G.A. (1980). Five years of international research with GIFT: An instrument for the identification of creativity. *Journal of Creative Behavior, 14,* 35–46.

Roe, A. (1952). *The making of a scientist.* New York: Dodd, Mead.

Rogers, C.R. (1961). *On becoming a person.* Boston: Houghton Mifflin.

Rosen, C.E. (1974). The effects of sociodramatic play on problem solving behavior among culturally disadvantaged preschool children. *Child Development, 45,* 920–927.

Rothenberg, A. (1983). Psychopathology and creative cognition: A comparison of hospitalized patients, Nobel laureates and controls. *Archives of General Psychiatry, 40,* 937–942.

Rothenberg, A. (1988). Creativity and the homospatial process: Experimental studies. *Psychiatric Clinics of North America, 11,* 443–460.

Rothenberg, A. (1990). Creativity, mental health, and alcoholism. *Creativity Research Journal, 31,* 179–201.

Rump, E.E. (1979). *Divergent thinking, aesthetic preferences and orientation towards Arts and Sciences.* Unpublished doctoral dissertation, University of Adelaide.

Runco, M.A. (1989). Parents' and teachers' ratings of the creativity of children. *Journal of Social Behavior and Personality, 4,* 73–83.

Runco, M.A. (1990). Implicit theories and creative ideation. In M.A. Runco & R.S. Albert (Eds.), *Theories of creativity* (pp. 234–252). Newburgy Park, CA: Sage Publications.

Runco, M.A. (Ed.). (1991). *Divergent thinking.* Norwood, NJ: Ablex Publishing Corp.

Runco, M.A. (in press). Children's divergent thinking and creative ideation. *Developmental Review.*

Runco, M.A., & Albert, R.S. (1986). The threshold hypothesis regarding creativity and intelligence: An empirical test with gifted and nongifted children. *Creative Child and Adult Quarterly, 11,* 212–218.

Rutter, M. (1979). *Fifteen thousand hours.* London: Open Books.

Sadek, A.A.M. (1986). The nature of musical creativity among Egyptian students. In A.J. Cropley, K.K. Urban, H. Wagner, & W.H. Wieczerkowski (Eds.), *Giftedness: A continuing worldwide challenge* (pp. 204–207). New York: Trillium.

Sappington, A.A., & Farrar, W.E. (1982). Brainstorming v. critical judgment in the generation of solutions which conform to certain reality constraints. *Journal of Creative Behavior, 16*, 68–73.

Scheliga, J. (1988). *Musik machen und die Förderung von Kreativität*. Unpublished master's thesis, University of Hamburg.

Schoppe, K.-J. (1975). *Verbaler Kreativitätstest. Ein Verfahren zur Erfassung verbal-produktiver Kreativitätsmerkmale*. Göttingen: Hogrefe.

Schubert, D.S. (1973). Intelligence as necessary but not sufficient for creativity. *Journal of Genetic Psychology, 112*, 45–47.

Schubert, D.S. (1975). Creativity and the ability to cope. *Creative Psychiatry, 5*, 1–24.

Schubert, D.S.P., Wagner, H.E., & Schubert, H.J.P. (1988). Family constellation and creativity: Increased quantity of creativity among last-borns. *Creative Child and Adult Quarterly, 13*, 97–103.

Schwarzkopf, D. (1981). *Selbstentfaltung durch kreatives Gestalten*. Unpublished master's thesis, University of Hamburg.

Sierwald, W. (1989, September). *Kreative Hochbegabung—Identifikation, Entwicklung und Förderung kreativ Hochbegabter*. Paper presented at 2nd Meeting of the Section Educational Psychology of the German Psychological Society, Munich.

Simonton, D.K. (1988). *Scientific genius. A psychology of science*. Cambridge, UK: Cambridge University Press.

Stanley, J.C. (1984). Use of general and specific aptitude measures in identification: Some principles and certain cautions. *Gifted Child Quarterly, 28*, 177–180.

Stein, A., & Stein, H. (1984). *Kreativität—psychoanalytische und philosophische Aspekte*. Munich: Johannes Bermann.

Sternberg, R.J. (1985). *Beyond IQ: A triarchic theory of human intelligence*. New York: Cambridge University Press.

Sternberg, R.J. (1988). A three-facet model of creativity In R.J. Sternberg (Ed.), *The nature of creativity* (pp. 125–147). New York: Cambridge University Press.

Sternberg, R.J. (1991). Theory-based testing of intellectual abilities: Rationale for the Sternberg Triarchic Ability Test. In H.A.H. Rowe (Ed.), *Intelligence: Reconceptualization and measurement* (pp. 183–201). Hillsdale, NJ: Erlbaum.

Suchmann, J.R. (1961). Inquiry training: Building skills for autonomous discovery. *Merrill-Palmer Quarterly, 7*, 147–169.

Sutton-Smith, B. (1967). The role of play in cognitive development. *Young Children, 22*, 361–370.

Taylor, C.W., & Barron, F.X. (Eds.). (1963). *Scientific creativity: Its recognition and development*. New York: Wiley.

Taylor, C.W., & Ellison, R.L. (1978). *Manual for Alpha Biographical Inventory—Form U*. Salt Lake City, UT: Institute for Behavioral Research in Creativity.

Taylor, I.A. (1975). An emerging view of creative actions. In I.A. Taylor & J.W. Getzels (Eds.), *Perspectives in creativity*. Chicago: Aldine.

Terman, L.M. (1925). *Genetic studies of genius*. Palo Alto, CA: Stanford University Press.

Torrance, E.P. (1962). *Guiding creative talent.* Englewood Cliffs, NJ: Prentice-Hall.

Torrance, E.P. (1963). *Education and the creative potential.* Minneapolis: University of Minnesota Press.

Torrance, E.P. (1964). Education and creativity. In C.W. Taylor (Ed.), *Creativity: Progress and potential* (pp. 49–128). New York: McGraw Hill.

Torrance, E.P. (1965). *Rewarding creative behavior.* Englewood Cliffs, NJ: Prentice-Hall.

Torrance, E.P. (1972). Predictive validity of the Torrance Test of Creative Thinking. *Journal of Creative Behavior, 32,* 401–405.

Torrance, E.P. (1974). *Torrance Tests of Creative Thinking.* Bensenville, IL: Scholastic Testing Services.

Torrance, E.P. (1980). Growing up creatively gifted: A 22-year longitudinal study. The creative child and adult. *Creative Child and Adult Quarterly, 5* (3), 148–150, 170.

Torrance, E.P., & Hall, L.K. (1980). Assessing the further reaches of creative potential. *Journal of Creative Behavior, 14,* 1–19.

Torrance, E.P., Torrance, J.P., Williams, S.J., & Horng, R.-Y. (1978). *Handbook for training future problem solving teams.* Athens, GA: Programs for Gifted and Talented Children, Department of Educational Psychology, University of Georgia.

Toynbee, A. (1962). Has America neglected its creative minority? *California Monographs, 72,* 7–10.

Treffinger, D.J., & Gowan, I.C. (1971). An update representative list of methods and educational materials for stimulating creativity. *Journal of Creative Behavior, 6,* 236–252.

Treffinger, D.J., Isaksen, S.G., & Firestein, R.L. (1983). Theoretical perspective on creative learning and its facilitation. *Journal of Creative Behavior, 17,* 9–17.

Urban, K.K., & Jellen, H. (1986). Assessing creative potential via drawing production: The Test for Creative Thinking—Drawing Production (TCT-DP). In A.J. Cropley, K.K. Urban, H. Wagner, & W.H. Wieczerkowski (Eds.), *Giftedness: A continuing worldwide challenge* (pp. 163–169). New York: Trillium.

Vaughan, M.M. (1971). An examination of musical process as related to creative thinking. *Journal of Research in Music Education, 19,* 337–341.

Wallach, M.A. (1970). Creativity. In P.H. Mussen (Ed.), *Carmichael's manual of child psychology* (pp. 1211–1272). New York: Wiley.

Wallach, M.A. (1985). Creativity testing and giftedness. In F.D. Horowitz & M. O'Brien (Eds.), *The gifted and talented: Developmental perspectives* (pp. 99–124). Washington, DC: American Psychological Association.

Wallach, M.A., & Kogan, N. (1965). *Modes of thinking in young children.* New York: Holt, Rinehart and Winston.

Wallach, M.A., & Wing, C.W. (1969). *The talented student.* New York: Holt, Rinehart and Winston.

Wallas, G. (1926). *The art of thought.* New York: Harcourt Brace.

Weeks, D.J., & Ward, K. (1988). *Eccentrics. The scientific investigation.* Stirling, UK: Stirling University Press.

Weisberg, R.W. (1986). *Creativity.* New York: Freeman.

Williams, F.E. (1976a). Intellectual creativity and the teacher. In W.R. Lett (Ed.), *Creativity and education*. Melbourne, Australia: Australian International Press and Publications.

Williams, F.E. (1976b). Encouraging your child's creative potential. In W.R. Lett (Ed.), *Creativity and education*. Melbourne, Australia: Australian International Press and Publications.

Williams, F.E. (1976c). Is creativity an innovation in education? In W.R. Lett (Ed.), *Creativity and education*. Melbourne, Australia: Australian International Press and Publications.

Yager, R.E. (1989). Development of student creative skills: A must for science education. *Creativity Research Journal, 2*, 196–203.

Yamamoto, K. (1965). Effects of restriction of range and test unreliability on correlation between measures of intelligence and creative thinking. *British Journal of Educational Psychology, 35*, 300–305.

Zajonc, R.B. (1965). Social facilitation. *Science, 149*, 269–274.

Zarnegar, A., Hocevar, D., & Michael, W.B. (1988). Components of original thinking in gifted children. *Educational and Psychological Measurement, 48*, 5–16.

Zha, Z. (1986). A study of the mental development of supernormal children in China. In A.J. Cropley, K.K. Urban, H. Wagner, & W.H. Wieczerkowski (Eds.), *Giftedness: A continuing worldwide challenge* (pp. 31–33). New York: Trillium.

Ziv, A. (1976). Procedures to increase some aspects of creativity. *Journal of Educational Psychology, 68*, 318–322.

AUTHOR INDEX

Subject Index